Masters track & field athletes.
Redefining the limits of age one jump, throw, and race at a time.

BANKED TRACK.
USATF MASTERS INDOOR NATIONALS.
ALBUQUERQUE, NEW MEXICO. 2016.

RACING AGE

Photographs and text by Angela Jimenez

For my mom, Polly, who loves a good race.
and
For my dad, Jacques, who has crossed the finish line.

LEFT: ANGELA, 5.
BIRTHDAY PARTY RELAY RACES.
STAMFORD, CONNECTICUT. 1980.

RIGHT: ANGELA, 21.
HEPTATHLON HIGH JUMP.
IVY LEAGUE HEPTAGONALS.
NEW HAVEN, CONNECTICUT. 1997.

PHOTOS BY JACQUES JIMENEZ

As a kid, I loved to run.

At my August backyard birthday parties, I would host relay races with my friends. My happy place was racing barefoot across the yard, the smell of fresh-cut grass stinging my nose.

I was always an athlete. In college, I was co-captain of the track & field team at the University of Pennsylvania, where I competed in the heptathlon (a multi-event comprised of running, jumping, and throwing events). Then, my definition of competition was achieving my body's peak lifetime performance. When you are young, you think being young is the best thing in the world. I thought I was the best I would ever be and that I still wasn't good enough to have a professional career. I had to move on. I hung up my track spikes and went to journalism school.

A decade later, I was a thirty-two-year-old freelance photojournalist on an assignment for *The New York Times* in Manhattan. I met a doctor who was competing on the masters track & field circuit. I had heard something about sports with divisions for older athletes. He said I should check out an upcoming National Senior Games meet in Kentucky. So, I did.

I tossed a tent in the trunk of my car and drove down to photograph the meet for a few days. I was accustomed to shooting with a digital SLR camera, but I had an instinct to borrow a friend's Hasselblad 503CX. I chose black & white medium format (square) film with this older-fashioned camera. I had chosen a slower, more deliberate process using this older camera body. I had twelve frames per roll, no light meter and a crank to manually advance the film. It felt metaphorically harmonious with these athletes, who were working with their own older bodies.

I was intrigued for a few reasons. An aging athlete myself, I'd taken up yoga and acrobatics but I often wondered how, or if, my track & field career related to my life and work. And I had been thinking a lot about aging. My parents were getting older — my dad had been diagnosed with Parkinson's disease a few years earlier — and I was watching them grapple with the evolution. I was frustrated by the stereotypical depictions of senior citizens as frail or cute. I wanted my photos to rebel against cliché.

However, I had to admit that the masters track & field athletes *were* cute — so full of character and energy. But it was their fierce competitive intensity that took me by surprise. Honestly, I didn't understand it. What motivated them? What did winning mean to them? Why did it matter? I felt uncomfortable, even scared, watching these older bodies fly down the track. What if they fell? Yet I understood that I needed to photograph them for what they were — serious athletes — not as a novelty act. I had far more questions than answers and that is what kept me coming back.

I learned how the sport works: athletes age thirty-five and older compete in five-year age increments against their peers. So, an eighty-year-old woman competes in the W80 division with female athletes aged eighty to eighty-four. As soon as she turns eighty-five, she moves into the W85 division, competing against other women aged eighty-five to eighty-nine. Every five years, an athlete becomes the young kid again. There are medals and records in each age division and in each event. The measurements of winning and success are unlike what we experience as young athletes.

Few sports concretely measure the capability of the human body like track & field does: How fast can you run? How high can you jump? How far can you throw? This population of masters track & field athletes is creating a literal record of the evolving abilities of the aging human body. How fast can a man sprint the 100 meters at age seventy-five? At eighty? At ninety? What will that look like fifty or one hundred years from now?

I became interested in the trends of population demographics and aging. For instance, American life expectancy jumped thirty years between 1900 and 2013, from forty-nine to seventy-nine years. Decreasing infant mortality and other factors played a big part in that shift. But, if you survived to age sixty-five in 1900, you could only expect to live another eleven years. If you survived to age sixty-five in 2013, you could expect to live an additional nineteen years.[1] What will we do with all our extra golden years?

Our global population is aging. It's not just the baby boomers in the United States. The world population of people over eighty-five will increase by 355% between 2010 and 2050. A one-hundred-year-old person will become 1000% more common. (In contrast, during that same time period, the world's population of people under age sixty-five will only increase by 188%.)[2] How will science and medicine evolve to keep us alive and healthy into older age? How will we take care of our exploding elder population? Looking at masters track athletes, I glimpse a future where more of us will live long, active lives.

There are also disturbing racial, economic, and geographic discrepancies in life expectancy. Who has the privilege to age? Who will be able to afford to do cool things later in life, like becoming a masters athlete? Masters track & field athletes win very little prize money and get very few corporate sponsorships. The masters division of the sport is largely a labor of love, not just for the athletes, but for all the officials, volunteers, web masters, coaches, and fans who keep it going. Most athletes pay their own way, or raise their own funds, to compete.

Masters athletes are generally healthy, positive, and clean-living but the sport is not without those who transgress doping laws. There is little financial incentive to win, yet each year there are a few athletes who are banned or suspended for taking performance-enhancing substances. Like in the professional sport, masters athletes are increasingly subject to drug tests by the U.S. Anti-Doping Agency and World Anti-Doping Agency, at regional, national, and international competitions.[3] Athletes file what are called therapeutic use exemptions, doctor-verified letters for medications that are on the banned substance list. Ferreting out masters who dope for competitive advantage is a challenge, as many older people take multiple medications for legitimate health reasons.

Meanwhile, the very definition of a natural human body seems in flux: In our golden age of technology and medical advances, what is natural? Both young and old athletes are modifying their bodies. In major league baseball, one-third of all pitchers have had Tommy John surgery on their elbows, to replace a UCL ligament with a tendon from elsewhere in the body. 7.2 million Americans are living with total joint replacements. Among American adults aged eighty to eighty-nine, 6% have total hip and 10% have total knee replacements.[4] People who were unable even to walk to the mailbox can now run again. We are already becoming a somewhat bionic people.

Most masters athletes are seeking health and meaning through sport: There is always another race to run. I was inspired interviewing elders about the great things they are doing now, rather than in the past. I wanted to share their life stories through the prism of their masters athletic careers. Their journeys encompass huge societal shifts over the last century. Older men are veterans of wars that kids study in their history books. Older African-Americans came of age during legalized, enforced segregation. Older women grew up with scant athletic opportunities. Despite longer female life expectancy, there are far fewer female than male masters track athletes, especially in the older age divisions.

This project is neither encyclopedia nor catalogue of the sport, though one is surely deserved. Rather, this is a documentary work that I hope captures something of the spirit and depth of these individual athletes. I have followed masters track around the world like a sub-culture, photographing in Italy, Boston, Pennsylvania, Maryland, Kentucky, France, Minnesota, and New Mexico. Some athletes I have seen only once. Others, I have seen repeatedly, all over the world. I made these photographs at several types of track competitions: the National Senior Games, the Penn Relays Carnival, USA Track & Field (USATF) Masters Indoor and Outdoor Championships, and the World Masters Athletics Championships (WMAC).

There are thousands of masters track & field athletes. Eight thousand competed at the last World Masters and fifteen hundred competed at the last USATF nationals. I chose to profile athletes over sixty, envisioning that age as a traditional juncture between working life and retirement. I observed how these athletic bodies seemed to rapidly change starting at that age, losing muscle mass and changing form.

After photographing for a few years, I put this project on the shelf from 2010 to 2014. That year, my dad, whose Parkinson's had progressed, died of a brain tumor. I watched his body waste away. My dad was more a man of the mind than the body, and I think he was always somewhat perplexed that he had a daughter who turned out to be such a jock. He was much more comfortable at a Shakespeare play than at the track. But he was, as they say, a good sport about it. One of the things he did was to take beautiful photos of me running. As part of my grieving process, I picked up my camera once again.

Last summer, two years after my dad's death, my intrepid seventy-two-year-old mom, Polly, and I went on an adventure to photograph the World Masters championships in France. My mom, a former field hockey, basketball, and softball athlete who was a devoted coach and fan during my childhood athletic career, was excited to watch the meet up close. She related to the athletes because she was at a similar life stage — they had retired from careers, had children, then grandchildren and some, like her, had lost their spouses. "I was in the middle of not knowing where I was going to be," she says. On that day, she was with them, at the track. "We were in the same basket."

In this society, we are conditioned to seek the magic bullet for a long, healthy life. The back pages of magazines and the margins of websites are replete with products promising to turn back time — or at least slow it down. There are lessons to take from these athletes, even though they are outliers. Very few of us are, or will ever be, masters athletes. Even fewer of us will ever be world-record breaking masters athletes. Personally, I don't know if I will ever run a race again. The inspiration I take from these athletes is intangible yet profound.

The morning of my fortieth birthday, instead of running barefoot relay races in the backyard, my mom and I went to the track in Lyon to photograph an eighty-four-year-old woman breaking the world record in the heptathlon, the event I competed in when I was in my twenties. Even if I never hurdle again, I want to approach my life with her spirit.

The first time you see these athletes, they are surprising. They don't fit into the categories your brain is accustomed to: *Old people aren't athletes. They belong in nursing homes, in wheelchairs. They certainly don't pole vault!* So it seems like a novelty, and you fixate on what isn't normal to you. A wrinkly body in a track suit. A grandmother throwing the shot put. A puff of white hair shooting skyward then landing. It is only in seeing something over and over again that you then start to allow those contradictions to exist. You get used to it, you accept it.

And then you start to see something else. An athlete, racing for reasons you might not grasp, against forces you cannot see. Racing age.

ROY ENGLERT, 86, OF VIRGINIA.
ONLY COMPETITOR IN THE M85 MILE (9:50.68).
USATF MASTERS INDOOR NATIONALS.
LANDOVER, MARYLAND. 2009.

STILL RUNNING INTO HIS 90S, HE WAS ON RELAY TEAMS
THAT SET THREE M90-99 WORLD RECORDS IN ONE MEET
IN 2014: 4X100, 4X400 AND 4X800.

MARGARITHA DAEHLER-STETTLER, 67, OF SWITZERLAND.
HEPTATHLON LONG JUMP.
WORLD MASTERS.
LYON, FRANCE. 2015.

STARTING GUN.
NATIONAL SENIOR GAMES.
ST. PAUL, MINNESOTA. 2015.

CHAMPION GOLDY, 90, OF NEW JERSEY.
GOLDY, A RETIRED METHODIST MINISTER,
IS THE FIFTH PERSON IN HIS FAMILY
NAMED CHAMPION.
NATIONAL SENIOR GAMES.
LOUISVILLE, KENTUCKY. 2007.

MASTERS 100-METER HEATS.
THE PENN RELAYS CARNIVAL.
PHILADELPHIA, PENNSYLVANIA. 2016.

CHAMPION GOLDY, NOW 99, COMPETES
THERE EACH YEAR. HIS ULTIMATE GOAL IS TO
RUN THE 100 METERS AT AGE 100.

JOHNNYE VALIEN, 82, OF CALIFORNIA.
SHOT PUT.
WORLD MASTERS.
RICCIONE, ITALY. 2007.

AT RIGHT: AT AGE 83.
USATF MASTERS INDOOR NATIONALS.
LANDOVER, MARYLAND. 2009.

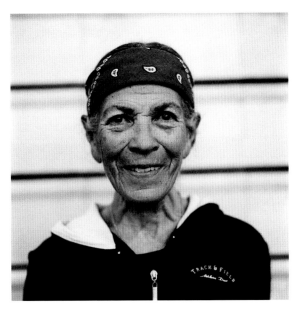

JOHNNYE
b. 1925

At the 2007 World Masters Athletics Championships in Riccione, Italy, Johnnye Valien is eighty-two. She is everywhere. First, stepping into the shot put circle, a bandana wrapped around her head. Then high jumping, surrounded by a small TV crew. Then long jumping. Then pole-vaulting. Triple jumping. Throwing the javelin. Then, the seven events of the heptathlon multi-event.

Finally, dizzy from dehydration, she stops and sits. Her health is fine, but she forgets to drink water. "I'm old enough to know that. But that's one of my weaknesses," she laughs. She has twinkling eyes and a slight southern drawl. "It takes much more training with the years as they go by. I can't just hop, skip, and jump and I've got it made."

As she has gotten older, there are fewer women to compete against in her age division. So, she increasingly relies upon her self-motivation. "I like to compete," she says. "Like today with that pole vault the [official] said, 'Why would you go on a pole vault when you know you're hurting?' I said, 'Because I'm a competitor.'"

"I even challenge myself, you know, life is competition," she says. "It keeps me going. Mmm hmm."

Johnnye spent a lot of her life not bothering to wait for the world to catch up to her.

She was born in Galveston, Texas. Her mother, Beatrice, was a dancer who worked as a maid and her father, John, was a baseball player who worked as a mason. He named his firstborn after himself.

"I was supposed to be a boy, and I was a girl," she says. "So my father raised me like a boy."

As a child she was always in motion — running, climbing trees, tap dancing, swimming, and doing gymnastics. She sat still for cowboy movies and little else.

She was a black girl growing up in the segregated south, thirty years before the Supreme Court ruled segregation unconstitutional and over forty years before Title IX revolutionized girls and women's sports in the United States.

Her family lived around the corner from an ice rink and Johnnye wished she could skate, "I saw all those little girls with their little tutus and their ice skates." Only whites were allowed in the rink. Only whites were allowed at the public pools. "No one ever explained that to me as a child," she says.

Her paternal grandmother, Elizabeth Pete, whom she called Mama, raised her in Houston in the 1930s. "She'd drag me to church every time I looked around." Mama sent her to Catholic school, and it was the nuns who introduced her to basketball and the thrill of competition.

"The nuns, even with their long habits, they played basketball and they coached us basketball. I won my first trophy at age twelve in seventh grade," she says. "We would travel to other cities and Louisiana for competition."

Johnnye enrolled to study physical education at Tuskegee Institute in Alabama, a historically black university founded by Booker T. Washington. There, she met athletic director Cleve Abbott. His ground-breaking women's track program won fourteen national championships between 1936 and 1955.[1]

Johnnye joined the formidable team, which included four athletes who made the 1948 Olympic team. Alice Coachman won the high jump, the first black woman to win an Olympic gold medal.[2] Nell Jackson, who ran the 200-meter dash, became the first black head coach of a U.S. Olympic team in 1956 (she also coached in 1972).[3]

After college, Johnnye moved to Los Angeles to study at UCLA's graduate program in physical education. There was nowhere for her to compete, so her track career was over (for the time being).

Looking for jobs, Johnnye was disappointed to find few opportunities to coach girls in sports. She got a job with the Los Angeles Department of Parks and Recreation.

She stayed for three decades, teaching dance, drama, and arts & crafts to the young and old, preschoolers to senior citizens. She used her position to create new programs, coaching volleyball and basketball teams and organizing track & field meets for boys and girls.

Johnnye enjoyed the wide range of people she met, and the work suited her. "You could wear pants," she says. "You didn't have to wear nylons and stockings. It was more relaxed." She considers her work with the Rec Department her proudest accomplishment. "I think I did something," she says.

I'm a competitor. I even challenge myself, you know, life is competition.

As an adult, Johnnye seized every opportunity to be active. Three times weekly, she went to the ice rink, determined to learn to skate. As a mother, she tried to give her three children access to things she longed for as a child. She took them skiing, camping, and to Europe on half-priced kids tickets. She put her daughter, Roxanne, on skis at 23 months. Skiing became a family affair: at one summit of the National Brotherhood of Skiers, a black skiing organization, Johnnye, Roxanne, and her grandson all won gold medals.

A lifelong athlete, she discovered masters track & field at age sixty-eight, when she read about it in the newspaper. Forty years after her last meet with her Tuskegee team, she laced up her spikes again. She has built a winning career, setting numerous American and world records. In 2001, she was named the USATF Masters Athlete of the Year, and in 2002 she was inducted into the USATF Masters Hall of Fame.

As a masters track athlete and a competitive ski racer, Johnnye has competed all over the United States and around the world: Italy, Australia, Finland, South Africa, Puerto Rico, Barbados, Mexico, Japan, Canada, New Zealand, and Argentina. Now, at age ninety, Johnnye's career is slowing, and she spends more time at her Los Angeles home. She is pain-free, takes no medication, but an inner ear problem has her struggling with her balance. Her last major meet was in Brazil in 2013.

She lives on her own, and her kids worry. Her son Robert James lives nearby and checks in often. "He drives me up the wall: 'Mom! You okay?'" Roxanne wants her to live with her, but Johnnye's answer is firm, "I'm not gonna be programmed!"

She decided to stop driving because people were shouting at her to get out of the way. "I didn't want to lose my religion, driving!" she laughs.

She has no intention of retiring from masters track. "That's my outlet," she says. She's not ready to be homebound. She rides the bus or walks, studies tai-chi, dances at church, and looks wistfully at her skiis.

Masters track has been a place for her to find compatible, active senior peers. Her neighbors are younger, but bedridden and alone. They can't keep up like her fellow senior athletes. She has outlived many friends. Nell and Alice, her Tuskegee teammates, are both gone.[+]

She sees changes in the world around her, some good, some not. She worries about the future for her eight grandchildren: "crime, shootings, immorality, drugs, marijuana dispensaries." She watched, disappointed, as a teenager stared at his phone during church. "People don't know what's going on around them. They're...what's that called? Texting."

Many of Johnnye's multiple American and world records have been broken. She still has the American indoor record in the W85 shot put and the world record in the W85 pole vault. In 2015, Flo Meiler broke her world record in the W80 heptathlon, the oldest age category for which a record exists in that event. But Johnnye doesn't dwell on the past, she is looking ahead: she's a youngster in the sparsely contested W90 division. She wants to make new records in the hurdles, triple jump, maybe the long jump.

She knew the late, great Olga Kotelko, a famous nonagenarian Canadian who still dominates the record books in the W90 and W95 divisions. Johnnye plans to make her mark. "It's not so much break the record. It's SET the record."

She hopes to compete again. Her vertigo is better when she walks sideways, and she jokes that maybe she will run a 50-meter race that way. For now, though, she is doing noticeably less.

"I would slow down, but I don't think I would stop," she says. "It's an ongoing life process, just to be alive. I think all the body functions, even the brain, need exercise. I plan on doing less body exercise or fitness and start concentrating — because that's what's slowing down, the old brain: memory, loss of hearing, and some of those things we can't change."

"As long as I think about it and concentrate on it I'm going to do it. Give it a try."

Yesterday, Johnnye says, she took a long walk outside for the first time in a while. She still can't get used to the drought-tolerant landscaping that is replacing grass and plants with cactus and rocks around water-starved Los Angeles. What she noticed were the familiar signs of life perservering, no matter what. "The grass will come up," she says, "through the tiniest cracks."

SHOT PUTS.
USATF MASTERS INDOOR NATIONALS.
ALBUQUERQUE, NEW MEXICO. 2016.

PENGXUE SU, 87, OF CHINA.
OLDEST DECATHLETE.
DISCUS.
AT RIGHT: WITH FAMILY.
WORLD MASTERS.
LYON, FRANCE. 2015.

DON
b. 1939

Don Isett, 76, is an engineer, husband, father, and champion pole-vaulter. He uses his mind and body, on a perpetual quest to fly higher.

"I do all kinds of things to figure out how to get into the inverted position," he says, "with my hands, shoulders, hips, and legs aligned perpendicular with the ground."

He plans his vaults days ahead, making calculations and pencil drawings to trace his trajectory over the bar. With meticulous attention to detail, he films every vault and watches the videos in slow motion, critiquing every jump.

At the 2015 National Senior Games in Minnesota, Don stands on the pole-vault runway, his sight fixed on the bar, set at 3.01 meters (9' 10½"). Beverly, his wife, sits in her usual spot near the mat. She watches every step of his approach, noting his precise take-off spots so they can analyze his vaults.

Don sprints down the runway and plants the pole, turning speed into height, propelling himself skyward. At the peak of his arc, his kinetic energy pauses at zero. For an instant as he passes over the bar, he is going neither up nor down. Once on the other side, he falls back to earth.[1]

It all happens in an instant. Then Don is back on his feet, exchanging high fives with his competitors.

"Thank heavens he's back," says Beverly, shedding a few tears. She confides she's been concerned about his recent performance decline. His confidence had been shaken in the preceding months by a torn meniscus, a hernia, and a shoulder injury. "When all that breaks down it devastates you, kills you," Don says.

Athletes generally peak in their youth, but Don has ripened with age.

He had an idyllic small-town Texan childhood. He played baseball and rode horses through open land with his friends, loaded 22s in their saddle holsters. Football brought him hometown glory. He was an offensive and defensive end the year the Garland High School team won the Texas state championship. He could still be just telling those stories of his youthful glory days, he says.

He pole-vaulted some in high school, but was a scholarship sprinter at the University of Texas. He didn't touch a pole for years, although he remained athletic all through his adulthood.

When Don and Beverly met at the office in the 1980s, Don was focused on taekwondo. "Karate, karate, karate," says Beverly. "And then when he was done with that, he was done. That's just his personality."

He got his brown belt, then moved on to white-collar boxing, a version of the sport for amateur white-collar professionals. Don laughs, "I have an attention span that lasts about eight years."

After he quit boxing, Don's engineering background propelled him to a more cerebral hobby, building and flying a two-seater plane.

Don fit his athletic career in alongside his work and family commitments. Together, Don and Beverly ran an engineering firm and raised Don's two sons from a previous marriage.

But by his mid-sixties, Don was in limbo. He and Beverly had retired and he was no longer flying. He took up running to treat his high blood pressure. As soon as he heard about masters track, it went from a hobby to serious interest. Don asked Beverly for a vaulting pole for his sixty-fifth birthday.

I just don't think I could bear to leave this world. I'm having so much fun.

Pole-vaulting was a new kind of flying. And you can't come back to football later in life, but it turns out you can return to vaulting.

He joined the Texas Express Track club and started training with Buzz Andrews and his son Chad, both former decathletes. Within a few years, he was vaulting a foot higher than he did in high school and breaking masters records. Don's personal best came six years into his masters career when, at age seventy-two, he vaulted 3.35 meters ($10'11\frac{3}{4}''$).

"I think the importance of it is, you enjoy it," Don says. He's not competing against the marks in the open, or professional, division of the sport. Masters is a different beast. "It's not that you're going to pole vault higher than anybody in the world, you're not. If you look at all the records in the different age groups, you'll see that they descend from very great heights to much lower heights."

"It's hard to do, it's hard to learn," he says. "But when you pull off a good one, it's a high."

Don and Beverly travel to a dozen meets a year. When he vaults, Beverly watches from her vantage point alongside the runway, just as focused as he is. "We're just a team, every day," she says.

Among pole-vaulters, Don has found a community of like-minded friends. "It's not like college meets, where you were cutthroat, just out to beat the other guy," he says. He sees the other masters pole-vaulters repeatedly at meets, and they feel like a family. "You're not hoping for the other guy to miss, you're hoping for the other guy to do the best he can," he says. "And he's helping you do the best you can. And we respect each other, we like each other. It's just a totally different approach to competition."

Now that he has found the sport and these friends, he sometimes worries about having limited time to keep doing what he loves. "In fact I wish I'd started sooner," he says. "I just don't think I could bear to leave this world. I'm having so much fun."

Don currently holds four American masters records (indoor and outdoor M70 and M75) and two world masters records (indoor M70 and outdoor M75). "It gives you a sense of self-worth, knowing that you jumped higher than anybody in the world and you didn't even do it in college," Don says.

Don's yearly personal best heights have descended in the last few years. His best mark as a seventy-five-year-old was 10'6". At seventy-six his best so far is 10'3." He continues to win meets and set records, but his goal is to return to his pinnacle, that 10'11¾" vault he did as a seventy-two-year-old.

"I'm delusional," he says. "I can't believe that I can't get back. I know all the data says you can't, but I still think it's in reach."

We're just a team, every day.

There are dangers in vaulting, but Don and Beverly don't focus on the risks. Once, in practice, Don fell off an elevated runway during a vault and landed on his back. He rolled over in the mud, expecting Beverly to yell "*Are you hurt? Are you hurt?*" But Beverly remained seated calmly in her usual spot, with a book open on her lap. Seeing he was fine, she yelled his takeoff measurement to him — 8'6"! — so he could analyze later what went wrong.

Beverly worries more about her husband's disappointment in his performance than the possibility he'll be injured. "I don't care if he wins or loses," she says, "but I know it means so much to him, that that's what I worry about."

Together for thirty-three years (married for thirteen), the couple live on twenty-two acres in Anna, Texas. They relish the easy mornings of retirement, drinking coffee and reading the morning paper. They enjoy live music and hosting parties, and do KenKen puzzles to keep their minds sharp.

Despite a good engineering career filled with accomplishments and some other serious sports hobbies, Don wants his legacy to be his pole-vaulting career. Not just because he's stuck with it the longest, but because it's given him so much pleasure.

Despite what he says, he's not entirely delusional about growing older: "You know it's all going to go away," says Don. "Age is going to change your body."

At the 2016 USATF Masters Indoor Championships in New Mexico, Don won his M75 age division and was feeling good. That night, he and Beverly joined a big, unruly crew of pole-vaulters and their companions for a tram ride up to Sandia Peak, 10,000 feet above Albuquerque.

There, the couple sat in the middle of a long table, smiling amidst the din of boisterous conversation and pole-vault stories. A few hours later, the server came over to tell them the last tram was leaving.

Don and Beverly crammed back into the tram with the group. They hung there for a moment before the slow descent, suspended in mid-air, with the city lights twinkling far below.

M80 AND M85 DECATHLETES, IN THE DISCUS TENT.
FROM LEFT: NURRETIN SABUNCU, OF TURKEY,
VIKTOR KLYPIN, OF RUSSIA, JOSEF PAULUS, OF GERMANY,
AND PENGXUE SU, OF CHINA.
WORLD MASTERS.
LYON, FRANCE. 2015.

M70 PENTATHLON SCORE SHEETS.
LEFT TO RIGHT: 60-METER HURDLES,
LONG JUMP AND SHOT PUT RESULTS.
USATF MASTERS INDOOR NATIONALS.
ALBUQUERQUE, NEW MEXICO. 2016.

	60-meter hurdles	Long jump	Shot put	
951	(493)	(668)	(790)	
	13.89	3.91m	10.00m	
752	(413)	(684)	(655)	(0)
	13.53	3.62m	8.50m	
578	(461)	(578)	(539)	(0)
	16.25	3.26m	8.79m	
.80	(164)	(455)	(561)	(0
	12.43	3.72m	7.75m	
01	(722)	(743)	(536)	(0
	11.92	3.42m	7.07m	
04	(804)	(621)	(479)	(0

OFFICIAL'S FLAG.
M75 1500 METERS.
NATIONAL SENIOR GAMES.
ST. PAUL, MINNESOTA. 2015.

RITA HANSCOM, 61, OF CALIFORNIA.
POLE VAULT.
AT RIGHT: HEPTATHLON SHOT PUT.
WORLD MASTERS.
LYON, FRANCE. 2015.

RITA
b. 1954

Rita Hanscom, 61, a record-breaking masters multi-event athlete, is a learner. There is always something new to practice or improve upon.

The same is true with her job. As deputy attorney general for the state of California, she prosecutes entities (drug companies, hospital chains, HMOs, and doctors) who defraud Medi-Cal, the state's Medicaid program for low-income residents. When she wins, she often wins big, with recoveries ranging in the millions to billions of dollars. With each new case, she has to grasp a new set of facts and complexities.

Rita was eighteen in 1972, when Title IX passed. Growing up in Arizona, she was part of the last generation to grow up without the sports opportunities it created for American girls. She was a tomboy — playing tag and kickball at recess, and doing pull-ups with her dad in the backyard. Her family went hiking and on road trips.

Rita knew she wanted to be a lawyer, and she had no idea she would wind up being an athlete. In high school and college, she was focused on her education. She briefly tried out for the college tennis team as a junior, but the coach told her she was too old. In law school at Boston College, she ran a few marathons, barely finishing, but it gave her confidence. "That's where you start to think — if I can run a marathon, I can be a rocket scientist," she says. "It's a good thing to do."

While working for a law firm in San Diego in her twenties, she met her husband, Dick, a superior court judge, through a lawyer's running group at the YMCA.[1] Every day they would join a group on a five-mile run through beautiful Balboa Park. "We probably ran 1000 miles together before we ever went on a date," she says. They got married, ran a few marathons together, and, when they had two kids, got running strollers.

Dick, eighteen years her senior, had knee trouble and stopped running in his sixties. He continued to walk. Rita, who was in her forties, continued to run.

At age forty-six, looking for an outlet from her mentally stimulating job, she found masters track & field. The track distances and disciplines — hurdles, throw, jumps

— were brand new to her. She felt no pressure, no expectation. "In a way that's to my benefit," she says. "When I discovered it, it was like a whole new world. It was like recess, it was like play."

And she didn't know much about training. Her first race, she says, "I was running as fast as I could. I thought that was it. You couldn't get any faster." She started training with Olympic javelin thrower Franklin "Bud" Held and his wife Nadine O'Connor, a masters athlete twelve years her senior. She discovered she *could* get faster! Much faster.

Rita started competing in the multi-events — pentathlon, heptathlon, decathlon — which are one- or two-day competitions comprised of multiple running, jumping, and throwing events that are scored using an international points table. The multis offered her what she calls a "panoply" of things to try. "You didn't have to be the greatest at anything. You just have to be moderately good," Rita says. What matters in the multis, though, is the sum of the parts. And Rita has turned out to be great at it. Her first heptathlon, she broke an American record.

Then she kept trying new things, including what she calls "the one deadly event:" the pole vault. Her dad had vaulted in the military. She remembers pole-vaulting with him a little in the backyard growing up. "Your life is made up of the choices and experiences you make. It gets easier to say 'no' as you get older," she says. "I want my response to be 'yes' for doing things."

Pole vault is a specialized passion, and a relatively new event for women. International track & field has recognized world pole vault records for men since 1912,[2] but for women only since 1994.[3] The event is one of the main differences between the women's and men's multi-events. The heptathlon, historically for women, has seven events and does not include the pole vault. Like with many gendered discrepancies in sports, there was a sexist assumption at play: Women don't have the upper body strength to pole-vault.

Today, women's decathlons (the ten-event contest which is traditionally for men) are occasionally contested. Rita, the constant learner, decided to go for it: She holds the American outdoor W50 and W55 decathlon records. "You need to look back on it and say, 'I did this, I tried that,'" she says. "The older you get, the tougher it's going to be to do it."

The stars aligned in 2009, when she was fifty-five years old. She competed in the World Masters Athletic Championships in Finland, and set her first world record in the W55 heptathlon. She was selected as the World Masters Athlete of the Year. She flew to Monaco for a fancy gala where she met and chatted with Prince Albert and mingled with elite Olympic athletes. "I felt like Cinderella," says Rita.

Rita, who now coaches herself, has continued to break records. She holds the American outdoor heptathlon records in the W50, W55, and W60 divisions. At fifty-seven, she broke the American indoor W55 heptathlon record. She was inducted into the USATF Masters Hall of Fame in 2012. In 2015, she broke her second outdoor world record, in the W60 heptathlon.

Her records are great milestones, but some have already fallen. That's just part of the process, part of the progress of the sport. You break records. Then your records get broken.

In February of 2016, Rita's husband died. They'd been married thirty-three years. She says losing him makes it harder to think about training, or to find the same enthusiasm she usually feels for competing. "What's foremost in my mind is trying to cope with the loss of my husband," she says.

"As time goes on, it's not going to be a challenge," she says. "It's a temporary thing. I recognize that."

In life, and in track & field, there is always another new thing to learn. You learn how good it feels to win. And how hard it is to lose, whether it is a race or someone you love.

AXEL MAGNUSSON, 86, OF SWEDEN.
LONG JUMPER.
WORLD MASTERS.
RICCIONE, ITALY. 2007.

NOLAN SHAHEED, 66, OF CALIFORNIA.
DISTANCE RUNNER.
USATF MASTERS INDOOR NATIONALS.
ALBUQUERQUE, NEW MEXICO. 2016.

NOLAN
b. 1949

For Nolan Shaheed, 66, trumpet player and distance runner, a track meet like a great gig. After a victorious show in the 1500 meters at the 2016 USATF Masters Indoor Championships in Albuquerque, Nolan seems to know and greet nearly everyone who passes by:

HEY YOU'RE BACK! IT'S GOOD SEEING YOU!

Nolan, a naturally happy and curious kid, grew up on Pepper Street, the same neighborhood in Pasadena, California, where Jackie Robinson grew up thirty years before him. He hung out with the Pepper Street Gang, which Jackie led as a youth, an informal group of neighborhood boys known for non-violent mischief, petty crimes, and sometimes just playing sports together.[1]

Nolan's parents had moved north from Texas. They worked hard to provide a good life for their three kids, and tried to shield them from the racism they had experienced in the south by sending them to a predominantly white private elementary school.

But, Nolan struggled in school. A teacher laughed at his curious questions and there were few references to the achievements of African-Americans in the classroom. His third grade science teacher praised the accomplishments of Einstein and Edison, then described botanist and inventor George Washington Carver only as the inventor of "peanut butter and sweet potato pie." It made Nolan feel ashamed.

"So, my life was happy when I was in my neighborhood and playing with the kids and doing what kids do," he says. "But in school and learning, I was in a big deficit."

In middle school, he asked his parents to buy him a trumpet. It was, he says, "the greatest thing that ever happened to me." He ran track a few years in high school, but music was his main thing.

He studied chemistry in college, which seemed a more solid career path than music. He kept playing music and running on his own. He explored black history, and went through a stage of self-realization. "It wasn't until I got to college that I really started learning about myself and who I am and how I relate to life that I started to stick up my chest," he says. He read about Egyptian, Nubian, and other African cultures and about the history of European colonization. He studied the teachings of Malcolm X and the Rev. Dr. Martin Luther King Jr.. He changed his name from Nolan Smith to Nolan Shaheed after studying Islam. "I was amazed," said Nolan.

His love of learning and teaching had been ignited. But, after college, it was his music career that really took off. He toured, performed, and recorded with some of the greats: Count Basie, Duke Ellington, Stevie Wonder, Diana Ross, Phil Collins, Anita Baker, Carole King, Tom Waits, and Freddie Hubbard.

In his twenties, he went on his first big tour, as Marvin Gaye's musical director. Marvin loved to play basketball, and some of the band members on the tour had run track in high school or college. Nolan would wager a whole week's salary on a race, betting he could run a mile (1600 meters) faster than a relay team of four band members (each running a 400-meter leg).

"I had the edge because I had never really stopped running," says Nolan. His teammates would go out hard and die fast, huffing and puffing. But Nolan would roll steadily along, his breathing as natural to him as playing a scale on the trumpet. He'd beat them by a few seconds, letting them think they had almost won. "It's a sucker's bet," he says. "I couldn't lose, you know, because I was doing like about a 4:10 mile then."

Nolan pauses his storytelling to greet another passing friend:

HEEEEYY. HEY MAN. YOU THE MAN!

Nolan continued to tour and play music in his thirties, and he started running in track meets. "I couldn't really wait to forty," he says. "When I turned forty that's when I started wrecking records and that's when I started really, really getting serious."

For the past three decades, Nolan has been setting the pace in masters distance racing. He currently holds seven world masters records in the 800, 1500 and mile, and seventeen American masters records in the 800, 1500, mile, 2000-meter steeplechase, 3000, 5000 and 4x800 relay.

In his fifties and sixties, Nolan continued to blaze through races, albeit a bit slower than he did when he was beating his bandmates on the Marvin Gaye tour in his twenties. He set the M50 world record in the mile in 4:25.04 and the M60 world record in the 1500 meters (just shy of a mile) in 4:24.

He was inducted into the USATF Masters Hall of Fame in 2004 and has been named the USATF Masters Athlete of the Year four times: 2001, 2007, 2008, and 2010 (co-winner).

His training and competition are integral parts of his life. "I think I compete mainly because if I don't, I don't know what I would do," he says. "I have a propensity for running and for running fast."

Nolan coaches himself, finding it easier to train alone: he finds he needs more rest between repetitions than younger runners, but wants to push a faster pace than most older runners. During peak training leading up a big meet, he trains vigorously. A typical workout might be twelve miles a day at 6:20 pace, followed by twenty 400-meter repeats at seventy-three seconds.

His music and running feed each other: he writes music in his head during training runs. "You know, I can have an idea, it pops in my head at mile three, and by mile five I have figured out the chord changes. By mile seven, I've figured out the structure of the piece and by the time I get home, all I have to do is write it down and notate it and I've got a whole song right there."

He follows an ascetic routine. He usually eats only once a day, in the evening after he works out, and drinks lots of water. During peak training, he says he only eats every other day. He weighs about what he did in high school.

The camaraderie among the masters athletes, he explains, is one of the most important aspects of the sport to him. Nolan shouts out to another friend walking by:

HEY MAN, YOU ARE THE MAN, HOW'D YOU DO? OK! I CAN DIG IT!

"When you go home and you're in the neighborhood," says Nolan. "You're just a sixty-five-year-old man and most men who are sixty-five can't do anything and they're full of diseases. Prostate cancer or diabetes or high blood pressure, particularly black men. So, no one really wants you to excel because your accomplishments are their failures, you know?" When he left home for this meet in New Mexico, one acquaintance warned him about the altitude, another that he'd probably hurt himself, another that he'd have a stroke.

Some doctors don't get it, either. A few years ago, Nolan, who rarely goes to the doctor, went to a cardiologist. He thought that, despite breaking numerous world records in his age division, something was wrong with him because his times were slowing down.

The doctor put him on a treadmill, and set it to a walking pace, trying to get Nolan's heart rate up to 160 beats per minute. "I try to tell him, you know, it ain't going to happen. Not walking," he says. "If I'm running a race then it will." The doctor diagnosed him with a low heart rate and gave him pills to raise it. Nolan didn't take them — his heart rate was low because he is in excellent shape.

"Doctors have never seen a person who is not sick, so they have no idea how to address someone who is healthy," says Nolan. "So, all the charts are wrong, particularly for older people."

Nolan realized he was just having a hard time accepting the advance of age and the slower race times that come with it. That's the beauty of the masters system, he says, where you age up every five years into an older age category. It keeps you looking up, not down.

His fellow masters athletes understand it. Like him, they have aging bodies, and are still competitive athletes. They share tips on training, hamstring pulls, kidney stones, heart valves, you name it.

"There's problems like everybody else, but we run through them. We fight through them," he says. "I think what we do is the greatest thing in the history of the world for old people."

As Nolan was telling stories, his teammate from the Southern California Striders walked over to tell him his team needed him to run a leg in the notoriously painful 4x800 relay. It was jarring mental shift for Nolan, who was sitting with his shoes off, relaxing and chatting:

OH MAN ARE YOU SERIOUS? OH GOD. ALL RIGHT. UH, THIS SUCKS, MAN. I THOUGHT I WAS DONE. ALL RIGHT. NOW I GOTTA RUN THIS AGAIN. THIS IS HORRIBLE. WOW.

"So, um, let me see, where was I?" he says, rattled by the news of an unexpected race. That's how running is. The thought of the next impending race consumes you. There is never too much time to dwell on one performance before the starting gun goes off again.

Nolan's short-term goals are to set more records and heal from injuries — a recent hamstring pull and a case of spinal stenosis, a condition that causes a narrowing of spaces in the spine and puts pressure on the spinal cord and nerves.[2]

These days, he works closer to home as a studio player, writer and recording engineer. He and his wife, who runs a piano school, have four daughters between ages twenty-three and forty-three.

He is coaching a high school girls' track team, and that feels to him like the most important thing right now. "All my life I was thinking that, you know, I want people to know me as the runner and as the historian and as the trumpet player," he says. "As I get older I find that I'm not afraid of death and I find that nothing really means anything. I find that the most important person in anyone's life is always a teacher, always, you know?"

"Girls in this country are not treated right, you know." Maybe someday, he says, his athletes will look back and think, "He taught me to respect myself. He taught me to respect other people."

Nolan stands up slowly, shaking out his long legs. It is time to warm up for that 4x800 relay.

EMILIA GARCÍA DE FONTÁN, 83, OF COLUMBIA.
AFTER THE 100-METER FINAL.
WORLD MASTERS.
RICCIONE, ITALY. 2007.

STILL RUNNING AT 90, SHE SET THE W90 400-METER
WORLD RECORD (2:46.56) IN 2015.

RIGHT: HIP NUMBERS.
USATF MASTERS INDOOR NATIONALS.
ALBUQUERQUE, NEW MEXICO. 2016.

SPRINTERS JOANN SAMPSON, 74, OF FLORIDA, LEFT,
AND BARBARA GARRETT, 74, OF SOUTH CAROLINA.
AT RIGHT: ON THE MEDAL STAND FOR THE W70 50 METERS.
NATIONAL SENIOR GAMES.
ST. PAUL, MINNESOTA. 2015.

THEIR FAMILIES SET UP CROWDFUNDING SITES
TO HELP THEM TRAVEL TO THE MEET WITH THEIR
HUSBANDS: JOANN'S GRANDKIDS SET UP THE
WEBSITE *JOANNSTILLGOTGAME.COM* AND
BARBARA'S DAUGHTER SET UP THE
YOUCARING.COM SITE *RUN, GRANDMA, RUN!!*

RICHARD RUCOBA, 90, OF ILLINOIS.
JAVELIN.
NATIONAL SENIOR GAMES.
ST. PAUL, MINNESOTA. 2015.

TOM PATSALIS, 87, OF CALIFORNIA.
COMPETING AFTER A DOUBLE KNEE REPLACEMENT.
AT LEFT: 55-METER SPRINT.
USATF MASTERS INDOOR NATIONALS.
LANDOVER, MARYLAND. 2009.

AT RIGHT: A YEAR EARLIER, GETTING TREATMENT.
USATF MASTERS INDOOR NATIONALS.
BOSTON, MASSACHUSETTS. 2008.

TOM
b. 1921 – d. 2014

It all started when Tom Patsalis, the son of Greek immigrants, was twelve years old. He won his first gold medal in the Junior Olympics. His proud school principal in Detroit, Michigan, paraded him around to show off his medal to the other students. It was his first taste of glory.

He was the best sprinter, jumper, and hurdler on his high school team and won the Detroit city championship in the long jump. World War II broke out and all other dreams were deferred. But Tom, who had played the clarinet and saxophone since high school, was an optimistic man. His mantra was, "Just don't let anything bother you and go on with what you want to do." He joined the Navy as a musician and played in military bands through the war, performing tunes like "Pacific Amphibious March."

After the war, he got a track scholarship from the University of Southern California. He just called them up and, like always, hoped for the best.

He was a member of the USC team that won a national championship in 1949. His best jump was 24' and he made it to the long jump quarterfinals of the 1948 Olympic trials, but did not make the team. He graduated in 1950, at age twenty-eight, with a degree in music and a minor in art.

With no further opportunities to compete, he built his life. He married his wife, Amelia Marie Valdez, known as Molly, and they raised three kids. Tom played music professionally, mainly with his own band, The Tom Palis Orchestra, booking gigs at hotels, festivals, and events. The band specialized in Greek and Near East music.

At age fifty, Tom read about a senior track & field event in Los Angeles. He saw that a guy he knew from his youth was doing really well in the long jump, and Tom was determined to beat him. "My main ambition was to get after him and try and break his records in the long jump," Tom said.

At his first meet, called the Grandfather Games, Tom won four events and set his first masters world record in the long jump. It was the early days of masters track & field, and Tom was a pioneer in the short sprints, long jump, triple jump, and hurdles. In 1977, he won three gold medals in the second-ever World Masters Athletics Championships, in Sweden. Between the ages of fifty-two and seventy-six, Tom set over two dozen world records.[1]

"When I was around sixty," said Tom, "that's when I was really my best." He set numerous records in his sixties, including a formidable M60 world long jump record of 19'11," which still stands three decades later. That is remarkable longevity in a sport where records are constantly being set and reset.

The USATF chose Tom as the Masters Athlete of the Year in 1987, when he was sixty-six.

Tom kept competing, and kept playing music in professional and community bands. At the banquets hosted by his masters track club, the Southern California Striders, Tom was known for taking the younger ladies for a spin on the dance floor — the tango, rock & roll — anything would get him moving.

Then, gradually, Tom's knees started to go. In his mid seventies, Tom took a hiatus from his track career. "I didn't want to have surgery right away," Tom said. "I waited until my knees were so bad that I almost had to get a cane to go up stairs."

Doctor after doctor told him there was no way he would ever be able to compete again as a masters track & field athlete. Tom, with characteristic positivity, was only mildly deterred. "I was discouraged, in a way," he said. Tom saw a doctor at his alma mater, USC, who gave him hope. "He's the only one that said there's a possibility," Tom said. "All the others said 'It's impossible.'"

He had a complete double knee replacement. "In other words, an open knee surgery," Tom explained. "It's not an orthoscopic surgery where they just go in there and clean a few things out." His doctor told him they used a special plastic material that, once set, would be even stronger than bone.

Six months after the surgery, the doctor took a look and said they had healed really well. He told Tom he didn't need to worry about his knees anymore. All he needed to do now was take care of the rest of his body. Tom had some shoulder problems, some high blood pressure, but nothing serious. He was still playing music in four bands, and wanted to compete again.

"You have to be positive all the time," said Tom. "When you do something, think of the bright side of what you're doing. That's the way you have to think."

In 2003, at age eighty-two, Tom was inducted into the USATF Masters Hall of Fame, an honor that could have just celebrated his past accomplishments. Instead, Tom got himself back up to speed, winning four American outdoor championships in 2008. His major concession to aging was that he gave up hurdling, but he kept jumping. He finally stopped competing at age eighty-nine, ending a masters career that spanned almost forty years.

On his ninetieth birthday, Tom walked briskly down the front steps of his home to a waiting limousine for a sunset drive down the coast to Malibu, a gift from his family. They hung a plastic "Happy 90!" medallion around his neck, and Tom shook his fists in the air like he had just won a race.

His grandson, Jason, filmed the video of him that day. Jason remembers his grandfather as a "competitive, open-minded and peaceful" man. "He was like a modern-day zen master," he says.

In 2014, Tom had a stroke and died several months later, at age ninety-two. He is survived by his family, his friends in the sport of track & field — and by one heck of a world long jump record.

W70, W75, AND W80 HEPTATHLETES.
MOVING BETWEEN EVENTS.
AT RIGHT: ON JAVELIN BENCH
(L-R) JEAN HAMPSON, OF AUSTRALIA, BRITA KIESHEYER,
OF GERMANY, AND FLO MEILER, OF VERMONT.
WORLD MASTERS.
LYON, FRANCE. 2015.

GEHRETT SMITH, 74, OF PENNSYLVANIA.
DISCUS.
NATIONAL SENIOR GAMES.
LOUISVILLE, KENTUCKY. 2007.

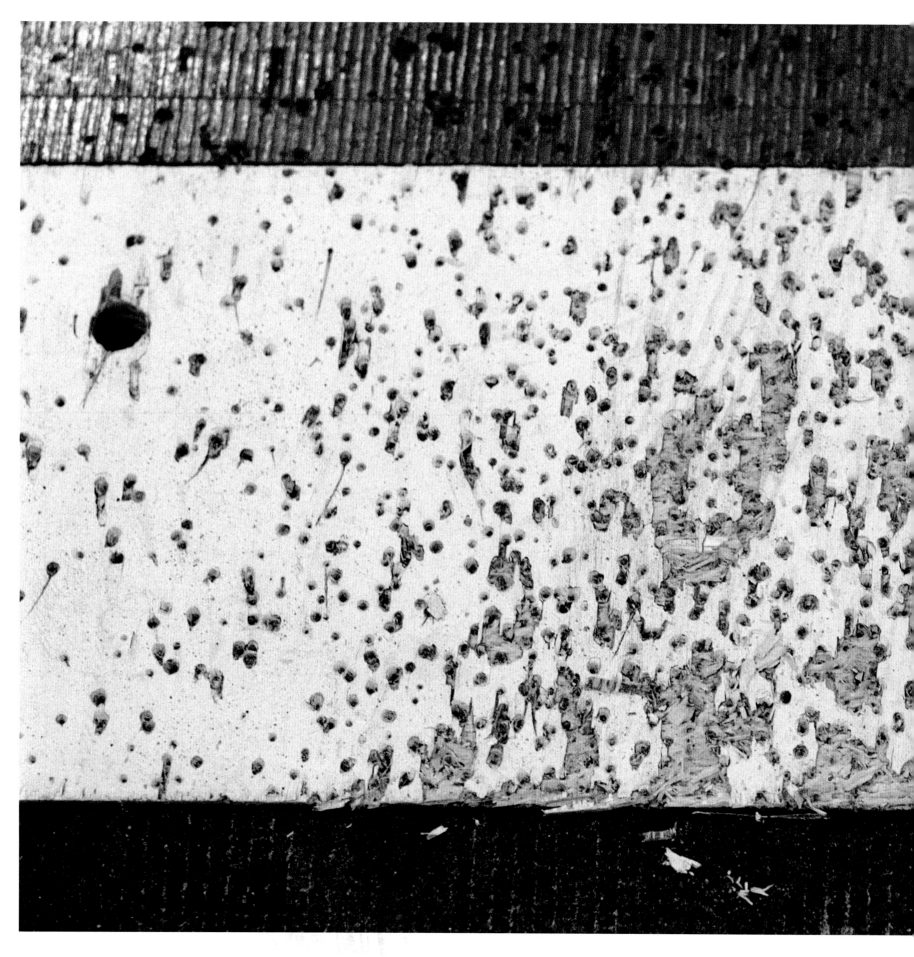

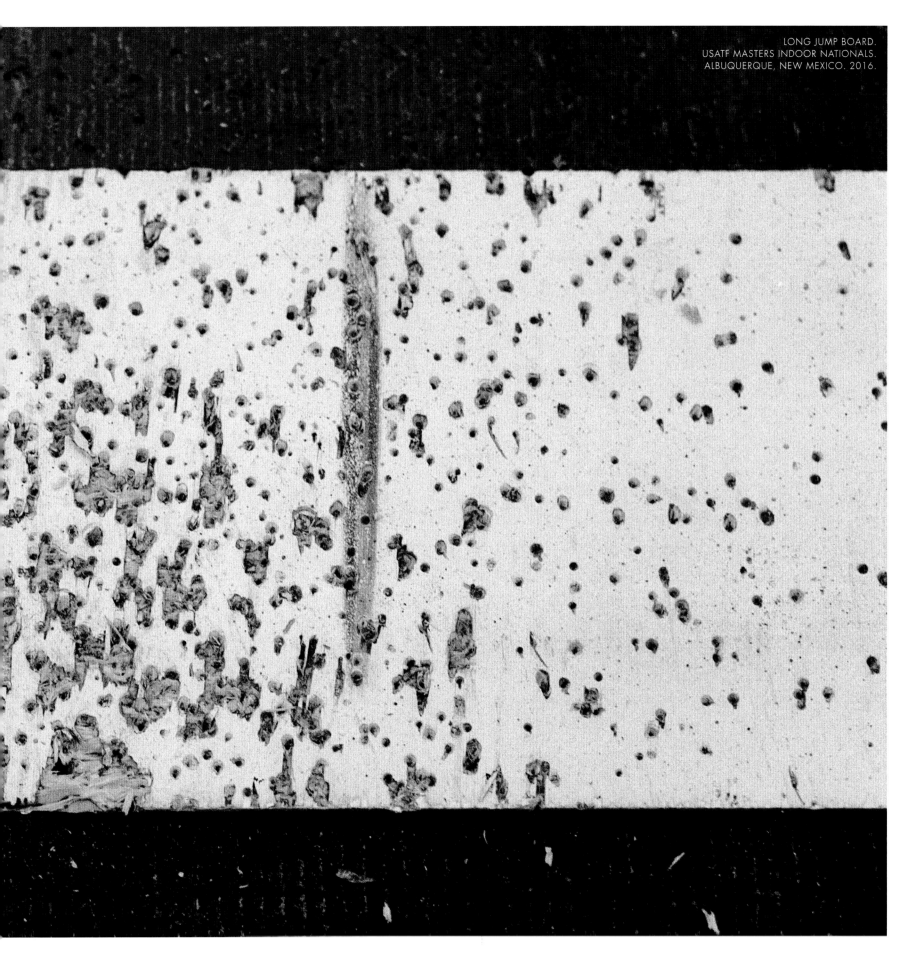

LONG JUMP BOARD.
USATF MASTERS INDOOR NATIONALS.
ALBUQUERQUE, NEW MEXICO. 2016.

KATHY BERGEN # 75.
WORLD RECORD. HIGH J.
1.25

KATHY
b. 1939

Kathy Bergen's first dream was to be a Brooklyn Dodger. "I wanted to play baseball," she says. Her favorite player was shortstop Pee Wee Reese.

Kathy, 75, grew up in an Irish family in Bay Ridge, Brooklyn, in the 1940s, a "total tomboy" surrounded by her older and younger male cousins. They played stickball between the sewers, Kathy hustling to keep up with them.

"It was a different time, a different generation," she says. The streets were the playground. She roller-skated and biked "everywhere," and played tag and ringolevio.

In high school, at the all-girls Catholic St. Saviour, it took her until junior year to make the 3-on-3 basketball team. (She spent a miserable year as a cheerleader in the meantime). It was half-court basketball: three girls on one end of the court playing defense, three girls playing offense on the other. "I couldn't shoot," she says. "But I was a tiger on defense."

Her mom loved track & field, and took her to see the Mill-rose Games at Madison Square Garden. People would fill the Garden for track meets then, and she remembers the great runners of the Santa Monica track club, watching a fast, young miler named Jim Ryun and cheering for "the great Irish contingent at Villanova."

Becoming a runner herself didn't seem any more realistic to her than becoming Pee Wee Reese. "It never occurred to me that I could do it," she says. "I mean, it wasn't even on the horizon."

"I had to go to school, I had to get a job, then it was get married and have a family and that's what I wanted to do," she says.

When she was seventeen, she met Bert, then nineteen, outside an ice cream shop in the neighborhood. "I needed a date for my senior prom, and that was it," she says. They dated while she commuted to college, got her economics degree, and worked for a few years. She was twenty-three when she got married. She stopped working, and she and Bert moved to Long Island and started having kids.

Kathy was heartbroken when the Dodgers left Brooklyn for Los Angeles in 1958. But Bert was transferred out to La Cañada, California, and, like the Dodgers, the family left for the west coast. There, she devoted herself to raising her five children.

She was thirty-two when she discovered a new love, tennis. "Oh my god. It's tennis. I wanted to play tennis 24 hours a day," she says. "And, obviously, I was very fast on the court and it made up for a lot of other inefficiencies."

She and Bert sometimes played doubles, and they met active friends through the sport. "I thank God for having a healthy body," says Kathy. "I go around the country when I travel and I see the round mounds of fat and, you know, I think, what kind of life do you have?"

All those shitty little boys who used to make fun of me – they're probably fat old men.

In the little time left over after tennis and caring for her kids, Kathy volunteered. She has worked in a hospital gift shop for thirty-two years. For a decade, she co-chaired a bi-annual fundraising auction that raised half a million dollars for her children's Catholic school. It was a big job that kept her busy every day for six to eight months out of the year, and it was hugely successful. It was the hardest thing she ever did, she says, until masters track.

The sport literally arrived at their doorstep when Bert turned fifty. "When you get old, you'll find out," she says. "AARP starts sending you the magazine." There was an article about the senior games. "So we went out and bought shoes. And it was like, this is fun!"

"I realized it was such a nice group of people. The men and the few women who did it, they supported each oth-er, they cheered for each other, they helped each other," she says. "I absolutely fell in love with it."

Kathy and Bert, who is a high jumper, began their new incarnation as masters track athletes. She joined the Southern California Striders club and started training, perhaps too vigorously. She taught herself the Fosbury Flop, the method of high jumping with your back to the bar. At fifty-seven, she herniated a disc in her back and spent a "wasted year" in recovery: "I was cooking, that was all I was doing for eight months." She gained ten pounds.

Eager to get back to the sport, and back in shape, she tried different events. She tried the shot put: "Got tennis elbow immediately." Then the triple and long jumps: "I don't like getting dirty." But, it turned out she was pretty good at the discus and the javelin. In a few years, she felt healthy enough to high jump again.

Kathy has been breaking masters records and winning championships since then, for 20 years. She specializes in the sprints and jumps, competing in five outdoor events (100 meters, 200 meters, high jump, discus, and javelin) and three indoor events (60 meters, 200 meters, and high jump). She currently holds eleven world and fifteen American records. In 2015, she and Irene Obera were named co-female USATF Masters Athletes of the Year.

Kathy has trained with coach Eric Dixon for the past seven years. He sends her workouts, tailored to her competition cycle. She has to find the facilities where she works out, which can be tricky for technical events like the high jump. She only practiced in a high jump pit five times last season before breaking an indoor world record — it's hard to find a pit to use.

Kathy works hard, especially on building her strength endurance. "This is where I feel most alive," she says. "I've never worked so hard to accomplish anything as I do in this. I can't believe how it works."

She eats a meat and potatoes diet, enjoys wine, and tries to keep her body healthy. She keeps herself on a schedule. "I'm very linear," she says. "Monday mornings is my tennis morning, so don't interrupt me. Tuesday, Thursday, and Saturday is workouts, so it's orange juice, my vitamins and the track. Wednesdays is when I do my volunteer stuff — meetings and crap like that. And Fridays and Sundays are usually nothing days."

Despite being generally healthy, Kathy has had her share of injuries. "I overstride a lot," she says. She has had various pulls and strains: hamstrings, quads, hip flexors, adductors, Achilles tendons. She's getting over a frozen shoulder, which she says was not caused by her athletics.

Kathy says a key to her success has been having great doctors. It took her awhile to find them. The first time she went to an orthopedist with track injuries in her fifties, he suggested, "Why don't you bike and swim?" She told him, "Because I want to run and jump." She never went back to him.

Instead, she found doctors who got what she was doing. "They don't make fun of me because I'm seventy-five," she says. "They say, 'Ok. She wants to do it, we'll help her do it.'" For fifteen years, she has seen her physical therapist Sandy Sheklow. "He's in his late sixties," she says, "and he understands what I do."

"The latest record is my favorite," she says. After setting two world records at the 2016 USATF Masters Indoor Championships (she ran the 60 meters in 9.49 and high jumped 1.25 meters/4'1$\frac{1}{4}$"), she was drug tested. Drug testing for masters track & field athletes is becoming increasingly common at both national and world meets.

They give you a little jar for a urine sample, she explains, then a detailed questionnaire to fill out. One question seemed "hysterical" to her: *Are you pregnant?* "Not for thirty-seven years," she laughs.

Athletes also have to account for all the supplements and medications they take, and provide a therapeutic use exemption from a doctor if they take a banned substance for medical purposes. In Kathy's case, she reports all the supplements she takes: Calcium, Vitamin D, B Complex, baby aspirin. *That's it?* That's it. She's not on any medications, a rarity for someone her age. She wrote her kids and told them about her new records, and about the drug test. Her youngest wrote back, "Uh, did they test you for Chardonnay?"

"Smart ass," she replied.

At this stage in her life, what's most important to Kathy is to be a good wife to her husband of fifty-three years, a good mother, and a good friend. She spends time with her thirteen grandkids. She takes pride in the fact that her records are setting a standard that younger athletes will have to try to best. Recently, a younger masters high jumper told her, "You know, you're making it hard for us." Because they will have to come along and try to break her records. It was "a special compliment" for her.

Who would have thought that little Kathy Bergen, running around trying to keep up with her cousins in the neighborhood, would grow up to be a champion athlete? That people would be racing to keep up with her?

"All those shitty little boys who used to make fun of me," she says. "They're probably fat old men."

There is nothing like a bright shiny medal engraved with your new world record. Nothing quite like winning in the long run.

DECATHLETE JANIS MANKOVSKIS, 75, OF LATVIA.
POLE VAULT.
WORLD MASTERS.
LYON, FRANCE. 2015.

LOUISE ADAMS, 86, OF COLORADO.
SOLE COMPETITOR IN THE W85 5000 METERS.
WORLD MASTERS.
RICCIONE, ITALY. 2007.

LOUISE
b. 1921

"I came into the world fighting," says Louise Adams, who is ninety-four. "I was a tiny little baby and wasn't expected to live." Growing up in Ontario, Canada, her only sport was running from her family's home to her school, miles away.

During World War II, Louise was stationed at a remote base in Newfoundland with the Royal Canadian Air Force, the sole woman among three hundred men.[1] "I had a great time!" she says. She met her husband, John, there. They raised four sons in Colorado.

Louise, an elementary school secretary, found distance running in her fifties. At just over 5' tall, she seemed unintimidating — but those short legs moved fast, and she was competitive. Her short stature, she says, had a silver lining: "The guys had cute buns and my eye level was about there."

Louise won races and broke records in national and international masters meets for three decades. In 2001, she was inducted into the USATF Masters Hall of Fame.

At age eighty-six, her racing career ended at the 2007 World Masters Athletics Championships in Italy. Under a hot Italian sun, she stepped up to the starting line of the 5000 meters (just over three miles). Louise was the oldest woman competing, and the only runner in her age division. Her only competitor was herself, and the clock.

The starting gun fired and Louise circled the 400-meter track, pacing herself for twelve laps. Her small, slight body moved steadily around the large, empty oval. Later, she recalled how heavy her feet felt. Suddenly, Louise fell. She quickly pushed herself up and kept running. A few minutes later, she fell again. She rose, her lip bloody. The crowd was rooting for her. "Go!" they yelled, a palpable tension between willing her to finish, but not wanting her to fall again. Louise's face was tight with determination, eyes locked on the track.

Again, she fell. This time, she sat still as a group of young medics in military fatigues approached her with a stretcher. "I wasn't hurt or anything," she says, but the doctors kept her at the hospital all day anyway. "Because of your age," they told her. *Because you are old.*

Officially, Louise's 5000 meter finish was DNF: Did Not Finish. But everyone there witnessed the tough race she ran. Days later, she came back and won the 400 meters, again the oldest competitor. But the falling was a problem. After Italy, she retired.

"I enjoy life," Louise says. She has outlived her husband and her oldest son. She lives alone in the house where she raised her family. Her three sons call every day. She doesn't walk the neighborhood alone, for fear of falling. A home health aide walks with her.

Her gold medals are stored in a coffee table in her living room. "I miss it, because I loved it," she says of her track days. "Well, because I did so well, that's why I loved it." She's delighted to hear her American indoor record in the W75 3000 meters (15:41.66) still stands. "No kidding," she says.

Recently, Louise got a letter from an English sprinter with "great legs," whom she met at that last meet in Italy. "We knew we'd never see each other again," she says. They were slowing down, and lived far apart. She was delighted to hear from him, an old friend she met on the track, doing what they loved, under the hot Italian sun.

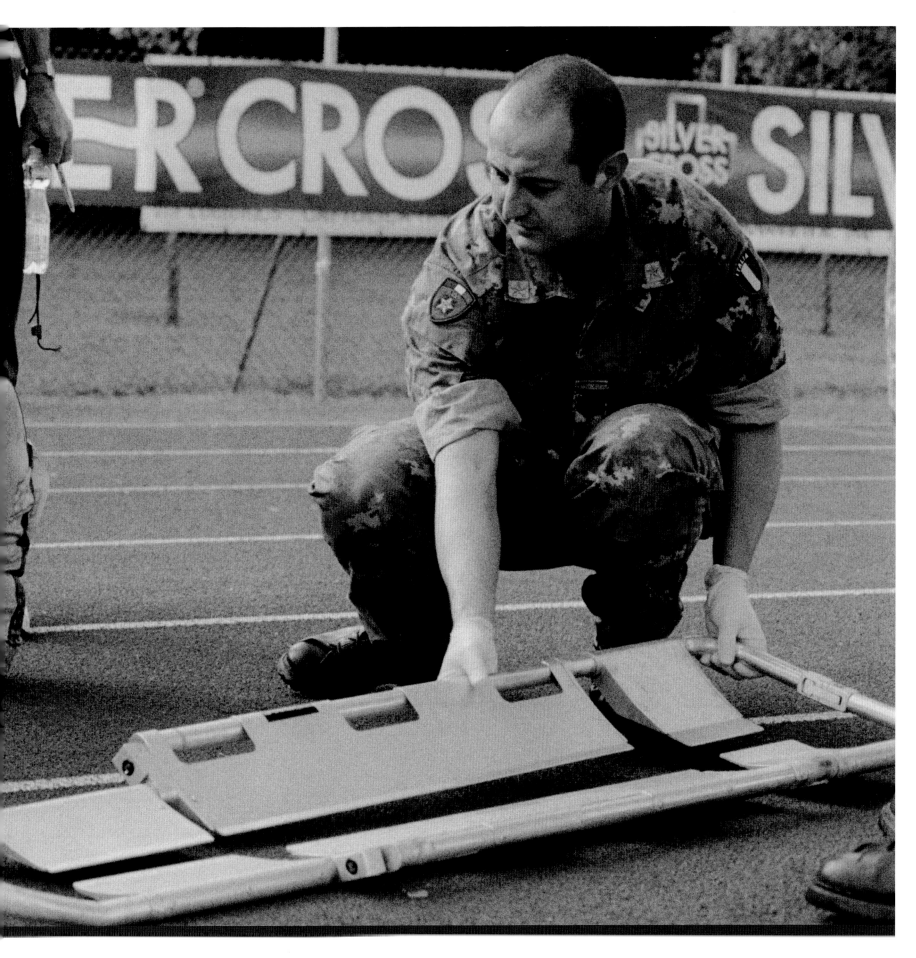

HEPTATHLETE FLO MEILER, 81, OF VERMONT.
WORLD MASTERS.
LYON, FRANCE. 2015.

FLO MEILER, 81, OF VERMONT.
AT LEFT AND RIGHT: WINNING THE W80 POLE VAULT.
WORLD MASTERS.
LYON, FRANCE. 2015.

TONY ROMERO, 73, LEFT, AND DAVID YEPA, SR., 74,
OF JEMEZ PUEBLO, NEW MEXICO.
AT RIGHT: TONY, 50 METERS.
NATIONAL SENIOR GAMES.
ST. PAUL, MINNESOTA. 2015.

DAVID & TONY
b. 1941 / 1942

Near Walatowa, the main village of Jemez Pueblo in New Mexico, the community has built a modern eight-lane rubberized running track. The small stadium is surrounded by pink and purple mesa mountain formations, under a big, blue sky. This is land where the indigenous Jemez have been running for centuries.

"Our grandparents, they were all runners," says Tony Romero, 73, a discus thrower and sprinter. "It's one of our traditional sports from way back from our ancestors. They taught us how to run, and we continuously do it."

Jemez (pronounced "Hay-mess") is one of the nineteen existing indigenous pueblos in New Mexico.[1] The Jemez have lived in strategically located villages, on vast stretches of land in the southwest, since the thirteenth century. By the mid-sixteenth century, the 30,000 Jemez were one of the largest and most powerful indigenous pueblo cultures. They carried news on foot, sometimes over marathon distances, across the high-altitude mountain mesas and canyons. Runners were their messengers.

Today, about 3400 tribal members live as a sovereign na-

tion on their land forty-five miles northwest of Albuquerque.[2] Competitive and ceremonial running remain a central part of Jemez culture. Here, kids start running at age six. The Jemez Valley High School cross-country teams have won nineteen state championships.[3] Eight times, Jemez runners have won the brutal Pikes Peak Marathon, a race up and down the 14,000-foot mountain.[4] Society group foot races, and other running ceremonies are held throughout the year.

Tony and his friend David Yepa, Sr., 74, a distance runner and friend since elementary school, both participate in the society group foot races. They discovered masters track & field through the Wellness Walk and Exercise group at the Jemez Senior Center, a community space for tribal members over age fifty-five.

"Nobody tells me to run, nobody asked me to run," says David, an 800- and 1500-meter distance runner who also does 5k, 10k and marathon races. "I love it."

The Senior Center has a common area with a television, a gym, a kitchen for daily, shared meals and recreational and fitness activities.[5] Tribal members have high rates of diabetes, high blood pressure, cancer, and obesity. "We need to be in good health. That's our main concern," says the Center's fitness coordinator David J. Gachupin, who trains the elder runners in the Wellness group.

About one third of seniors over sixty-five in Jemez live below the poverty level.[6] It's a challenge to engage the elders, who are juggling family responsibilities and financial pressures. Gachupin logs many miles in the senior center van, driving across the vast 90,000-acre pueblo to pick up elders for activities and meals at the Center, then to drop them back home at the end of the day.

David and Tony are part of the group of elders dedicated to running. Their group does morning walks, training sessions at the outdoor track, and distance runs on the trails in the style of the Jemez ancestors. "We just run cross country, all through our roads in our reservation up in Jemez. Everybody does that. We've been doing that since we were kids," says Tony.

It's one of our traditional sports from way back from our ancestors. They taught us how to run.

The runners compete in native competitions and at Senior Games track meets. David and Tony were among the few Jemez elders who qualified at the state level to compete in the 2015 National Senior Games in St. Paul, Minnesota. To prepare, they worked with a fitness trainer, doing cardio and weight workouts to get in shape.

For the elders, the opportunity to travel as an athlete is a huge benefit. David has been to every biennial National Senior Games meet since 2005 — traveling to Pittsburgh, Kentucky, California, Houston, and Minnesota. The only meet he missed was 2013 in Cleveland, for financial reasons. Minnesota was Tony's third nationals trip. Jemez elders are supported by funding from the Pueblo's tribally-controlled health department, and also raise their own money through fundraisers like bake sales and bingo events.[7]

"It's a great thing for me. It's a big honor," says David of the most recent trip, to Minnesota. He says he likes seeing the big cities and different ways of life. "We're way far away from home. We miss our family, but this is what we like."

At the National Senior Games, winning was not the only focus for David and Tony. Carrying on their ancestral tradition and serving as role models to the Jemez youth are equally important to them.

Tony finished last in his 50-meter race and sixteenth in the discus, but was upbeat afterwards. He says he is proud to represent the Jemez, and knows the tight-knit community will read about the elders' trip to Minnesota in the local *Red Rocks Reporter* newsletter. They will pose for photos in their track suits.[8]

"Now that I have been to all these nationals, I'm a role model for my Pueblo kids," he says.

David, who finished tenth in his 1500-meter race says, "I won a lot of medals, I won a lot of ribbons, which I'm very thankful to our Creator. Back home, almost all the people recognize us in what we do."

The Jemez have continuously lived in extended families for hundreds of years. There is no senior housing in Jemez and most elders there live with family members. David says he thinks about how his running might influence his family and the young kids in Jemez.

"We have to go back home. The people are waiting for us," says David, whose wife, four kids, three grandkids, and three great grandkids live in Jemez. "I want them to follow in my footsteps."

DAVID YEPA, SR., 74, OF
JEMEZ PUEBLO, NEW MEXICO.
1500 METERS.
NATIONAL SENIOR GAMES.
ST. PAUL, MINNESOTA. 2015.

M85 55-METER DASH.
USATF MASTERS INDOOR NATIONALS.
BOSTON, MASSACHUSETTS. 2008.

HEPTATHLETES FLO MEILER, 81, OF VERMONT, LEFT, AND
CHRISTEL DONLEY, 80, OF COLORADO.
REVIEWING FLO'S NEW WORLD RECORD SCORE.
AT RIGHT: FINISHING THE 800 METERS, THE LAST EVENT.
WORLD MASTERS.
LYON, FRANCE. 2015.

FLO VERSUS CHRISTEL
b. 1934 / 1935

If you had seen Flo Meiler, 81, and Christel Donley, 80, boarding a bus one morning in Lyon, France, in the summer of 2015, you might have mistaken them for tourists, on their way to a float trip down the Rhône.

The pair commuted together like two ladies on a summer vacation. But they were not on their way to sip wine in a café — they are USATF Masters Hall of Fame track & field athletes, and they were on their way to compete in the heptathlon at the World Masters Athletics Championships.

It was the first trip to Europe for Flo, who lives in Vermont, and she felt daunted by navigating the multiple competition venues in a new, foreign city. So, she and Christel helped each other. "I'm not very good at large cities," says Flo. "I'm not very good at buses or tramways. I was very nervous about that yesterday. In fact, I hardly got any sleep last night. If Christel had not been with me, I probably wouldn't have come."

The pair were the only competitors in the W80 heptathlon, the oldest age division for which a world record in the event exists. It is a grueling two-day competition comprised of seven running, jumping, and throwing events. Flo says people constantly question her decision to compete at her age: *Isn't she too old?* "No," she tells them. "As long as the Good Lord gives me my health, I'm going to keep going until one-hundred years old if I have to."

Flo and Christel arrived at the track in Lyon on the same bus, but from different life paths.

Flo grew up in Champlain, New York, where she tap-danced and played half-court basketball in a long skirt on her Catholic high school team. She worked briefly as a secretary, then married her husband, a B-52 pilot turned businessman. After several failed pregnancies and the heart-breaking death of their $3\frac{1}{2}$-year-old son, they adopted an English-Irish boy from Vermont, a French-Canadian boy from Canada, and a girl from Korea. "We have quite an international family," says Flo.

For thirty years, she and her husband were active, competing in water skiing competitions on Lake Champlain and playing tennis. Flo put her bubbly personality to use doing volunteer fundraising for the American Heart Association and selling Herbalife supplements, something she uses herself every day. "I'm very outgoing," says Flo. "I love people. I love to talk to them."

At sixty, she was playing tennis with her husband in the Vermont Senior Games and a friend begged her to come try the long jump. "I finished my tennis game and tried the long jump and that's all I had to do," she says. "From then on, I went to five events, then to eight events, then to twelve, and now I'm more like eighteen events."

Flo competes in the multi-events (pentathlon and heptathlon), and a plethora of individual events, from the pole vault to the 2000-meter steeplechase. She currently holds seventeen American and ten world records.

Christel grew up in Germany, where she competed in competitive club track & field from the age of thirteen. The multi-events were very different then. "We went 75-meters, we had a long jump and a baseball throw," she says. Instead of the heptathlon, there was the five-event pentathlon. The 200 meters was the longest run, because it was assumed women's bodies could not handle longer distances. "There was no 800 meters for women in the multi-events and we thought these people would collapse running two laps," says Christel.

Christel competed with her club team until she was twenty-nine. She remembers there was a woman in her forties, the mother of one of her teammates, who ran with the team. Christel recalls thinking it was "overboard" for someone that old to still be competing! Now, Christel is competing at twice that age.

She got her physical education degree, then coached track & field in the United States — ten years at a high school then twenty years at Division III Occidental College. She took a brief hiatus from competing before joining masters track in her thirties. Through the sport, she met her husband, Jerry, who specializes in the pole vault and also does multi-events. They are very involved in the sport of masters track and are probably the only couple who are both USATF Masters Hall of Famers — Christel was inducted in 1997, Jerry in 1999. Christel currently holds twelve American and three world records.

The record books show evidence of the rivalry between Flo and Christel. Just six months apart in age, they are often in the same age division, where they trade victories and vie for records against each other. "We try to beat each other," says Flo. "She's better at one thing, and I'm better in another thing, so it's fun."

For example, Christel has the American outdoor record in the W70 pentathlon, but the W75 pentathlon record belongs to Flo. Christel and Flo even share a world record, a W80 4x100 mark they set together as part of a relay team.

"There is a lot of respect," says Christel. "It is a pleasant rivalry." One of her roles, she says, is to keep Flo positive.

Their rapport is evident at the track. At this meet, they chat while they warm up, cheer for each other, and help each other measure the high jump bar to make sure the standards are right. Christel, a life-long athlete, has helped coach Flo, who picked up the sport late in life. "When I started," says Flo, "she helped me with my high jump. She helped me with my javelin."

In Lyon, Christel might have been the favorite in the heptathlon. Six weeks earlier, she had set a new world record, pending ratification. She and Flo lined up for the first heptathlon event, the 80-meter hurdles. The official raised the starting gun. "On your marks!" he called.

The women crouched down in their blocks waiting for the next command, "*Set!*" But it never came. Instead POP! The gun went off. They shot awkwardly out of the blocks, waiting to hear the double POP! POP! of the gun, calling the athletes back from a bad start. But that didn't come either.

So, they kept running, rattled and off-rhythm. On the last hurdle, Christel caught her foot and went down hard, face first. She got up and finished the race. "It affected me greatly because the command was so wrong," Christel says of the bad start. "We weren't ready when the gun went off."

"I felt really bad when she fell," says Flo. "That really hurt me because I wanted her to do well." Officials said they would let the pair rerun the race, but Christel decided not to risk a do-over.

I didn't sit in my rocking chair. I get out there and work out the pain.

"I found out I have a couple of bruised ribs," Christel announced after the race, holding a bag of ice. "Nothing is broken, apparently, but it's still kind of a minus." (A doctor later told her she probably had fractured at least one rib.)

Christel was frustrated at the slow hurdle time, nearly 600 points off her world record heptathlon pace, but there were six more events left in the multi. There was still hope. An eighty-year-old competing with a bruised rib, though? Surely no one would judge her for dropping out. Would she finish?

"Oh yes," said Flo after the race, with no hesitation. "She will. She's a go-getter. She will." Flo was right. Despite pain, Christel slogged through the competition, beating Flo in the high jump, the 200-meter sprint, and the shot put. Flo beat her in the long jump.

Finally, at the end of the second long day, the pair lined up for the dreaded last event, the 800 meters. They rounded the second lap, faces twisted in pain. Flo crossed the finish line first. They stood in the shade for a few minutes, heaving for air. Flushed with endorphins and relieved to be finished, they both pored over the results with an official. Flo's face opened into a huge smile. *Yes! She had done it!*

Despite Christel's fall, both women broke Johnnye Valien's existing world record score. But Flo, the winner with 5730 points, was the new world-record holder. For that day, at least, Flo was the best, oldest heptathlete in the world.

"Oh my gosh, I'm on cloud nine right now!" Flo says. "It's a good reward for the year and a half of training, five and six days a week. That's a lot of training."

"As the saying goes, records could be broken anytime," says Christel, who watched her record go up in smoke before it was even ratified. "So you enjoy it for a few hours or days or even a few weeks."

The two joined the younger heptathletes in the middle of the track, grinning for pictures. What would their advice be to younger people, watching them do this?

"I would say 'You see? It's never too late,'" says Flo. "I'm eighty-one years old and look what I did. I didn't sit in my rocking chair and say 'Oh, I've got a pain here, I've got a pain there, I can't do anything.' I get out there and work out the pain."

"Try it some time," says Christel. "We're doing it at our age and we will congratulate you." But take the congratulations in advance, she warns. By the time you are old enough to be like us, she says, "We won't be around anymore."

HEPTATHLETES CHRISTEL DONLEY, LEFT, 80,
AND FLO MEILER, 81.
80-METER HURDLES.
AT RIGHT: CHRISTEL FALLS DURING THE RACE.
WORLD MASTERS.
LYON, FRANCE. 2015.

ORVILLE ROGERS, 98, OF TEXAS.
MEDALS. **#USATF**
AT RIGHT: (L-R) HIS CHILDREN BILL, SUSAN AND RICK,
AND GRANDSON STEVEN CHEERING DURING
THE 200-METER DASH.
USATF MASTERS INDOOR NATIONALS.
ALBUQUERQUE, NEW MEXICO. 2016.

ORVILLE
b. 1917

Orville Rogers was born to fly. He was named after famed flight pioneer Orville Wright and he lived up to his namesake, flying as a commercial pilot until he turned sixty. Almost forty years later, at ninety-eight, he's a masters track & field star.

In high school in Texas, he was an average football player, but not good enough to make the team at his junior college. Once out of school, Orville enrolled in the military and was a flight instructor in the Army Air Corps during World War II, and later was a B-36 aircraft commander stationed in Texas during what he calls the "Korean emergency." After his military career, he worked as a commercial pilot. He and his wife, Esther Beth, raised four children in a devout Baptist household.

He was only moderately active in his adult life until his fifties, when he was inspired by Dr. Kenneth Cooper's book *Aerobics*. "I read the book and started running the next day," he says.

A preventive medicine doctor and a fellow military veteran, Dr. Cooper launched a fitness and health empire based on his "8 Healthy Steps" to living better: maintain a healthy weight, make healthy food choices most of the time, exercise most days of the week, take the right supplements for you, stop smoking, control alcohol, manage stress, and get a regular, comprehensive physical exam.[1]

"It was very inspirational, very challenging, and a lot of his theories were not proven at that time," says Orville. "But since then, it has been amply shown by scientific studies that physical fitness — which he describes as hard, long, and circulation system fitness, not muscular fitness — is conducive to long life and good health."

In 1977, Orville took mandatory retirement from his pilot career at age sixty. After retirement, he got even more physically active. In the ensuing decades, he has done multiple marathons, won medals in turkey trots, and climbed Mount Kilimanjaro and Mount Rainier. He was in his late eighties when he started looking at the masters track & field records. He noticed that the times were slower than his usual pace and decided to compete.

He and Esther Beth scheduled a trip from their home in

Dallas to the 2008 USATF Masters Indoor Championships in Boston. He was entered in the mile and the 800 meters. Esther Beth died two weeks before the meet.

"I knew she would want me to go," Orville says. "So I went ahead and went to the race." He says he "slaughtered" the M90 mile record by a minute and a half, finishing in 9:56.58. The record still stands.

He has been competing and breaking records ever since, often with an entourage of his large family accompanying him at meets. He sits with his family in the bleachers at the 2016 USATF Masters Indoor Championships in Albuquerque, an annual meet that always marks the anniversary of his wife's passing: "Eight years ago next week," he says.

His three surviving adult children — Susan, Rick, and Bill, all in their sixties — and one of his fourteen grandchildren, Steven, 32, were with him. (His oldest son Curtis, a marine helicopter pilot, was killed in Vietnam at age twenty-five). They unfurled a hand-painted banner that said "Go Orville Go!" alongside the track and cheered during each race. They unfurled it a lot at this meet, where Orville was the only competitor in the M95 division. He won the 60, 200, 400, 800, and 1500 meters, victorious just by competing and finishing.

Orville is all over the record books: He currently holds ten world and sixteen American masters records in running events ranging from the 60- to 3000-meter distances and various relay races, an unusually wide range of disciplines for one athlete. He specializes in the indoor competition. He and fellow athletes have teamed up to set standards in the 4x100, 4x200, 4x400 and 4x800 relays in the M90-99 age group, the oldest category for which records exist. (On one day in 2014, he ran on three record-breaking relay teams).

"I think my family has pretty well accepted my athletics," says Orville. "But my friends probably think I run because I can run. They have it backwards. I *can* run because I run."

Orville is disciplined and consistent. He trains at the Dallas-based Cooper Clinic health facility, which is operated by the Dr. Cooper whose book so inspired him. Orville lifts weights for thirty to forty minutes, three days a week, usually Monday, Wednesday, and Friday. He does runs of two to three miles at a time, averaging nine miles a week. "I enjoy it," he says of his training. "And I enjoy it partly because I know it's good for me."

Orville religiously goes in for his annual exam with Dr. Cooper himself, who is now eighty-four and still seeing patients. Last year, he had his forty-fourth consecutive annual exam with his doctor and mentor.

It hasn't been just health and ease for Orville. He's had a six-vessel coronary bypass surgery, lung surgery, and four different heart arrhythmias. His cardiologist at the Cooper Clinic, Dr. Nina B. Radford, understands he is an athlete and encourages him to keep competing. Orville's son Rick says he feels grateful to her "for being courageous enough to say 'Go do it,'" he says. "Because if the whole purpose in life is just to live longer, then maybe she should say 'Orville, you can't do this, because it poses a risk.' Well, life is a risk. Getting out of bed is risky."

At his most recent checkup, Orville was actually relieved when doctors told him not to run more than three miles at a time. He didn't really like running distances longer than that anyway. What limits him as he gets older, he says, is his aging body. "They have told me that I can run as fast as I want to," he says. "But I tell them 'But I can't run as fast as I *want* to!'"

Orville does not come from a family with unusual longevity. One of his grandsons traced the family ancestry back to the 1500s in England. His oldest ancestor lived to be ninety-seven. At ninety-eight, he is the "oldest one ever" in his family. And while many families spend most of their time cheering on their young kids — at soccer games, little league, karate tournaments — the Rogers clan spends a lot of time watching their oldest family member compete.

It has shifted the perception of life stage for his children and grandchildren. "I think it's kind of surreal, to be honest," says his grandson Steven, who is in his thirties. "Knowing who he is, it's kind of normal to watch him. Then you really actually think about the numbers, and it's almost...it's hard to believe." Maybe, like his grandfather, he can still be active fifty, sixty, or even seventy years from now.

My friends probably think I run because I can run. They have it backwards. I *can* run because I run.

At times, Orville's athleticism can be scary for the family. What if he gets hurt? But Orville has never asked for permission, so they don't have too much say in the matter. For his ninetieth birthday, he went skydiving and didn't tell anyone about it. At Thanksgiving, he called the whole family into the TV room after dinner and put on a DVD of his jump to show them what he had done.

"I've never said this to him," says son Rick, tearing up. "But what if he ran one of these races and collapsed and died at the end of the race? I'm like, 'Is that better than an ICU? Absolutely!'" Orville has gotten hurt competing and training. He has fallen while out on runs, and scraped his knees and elbows. One time, he fell at the end of a race and the emergency room doctors wanted to do a CT scan, despite the lack of any symptoms of a closed head injury. The family had to advocate against that decision.

"They were doing it just because of his age and I go, 'Did you tell them about yourself?'" says Rick. The doctors were picturing a typical scene of an old man falling in the bathroom. "You can't just look at his age and say 'You need to do a CT scan because it's an old person who fell.' You can't just do that anymore."

But with so few athletes competing the way he does at his age, medical professionals are still not used to working with someone like him. "They don't have books that deal with his age category, you know," says his daughter Susan. "He's setting a standard, and setting a pretty high one."

Orville finds meaning in his faith. "I credit my success in life, not only just in running but in every way, with my belief in the Lord Jesus Christ. And I'm fortunate, I guess, that He gave me the ability to run, and that I had the notion to develop that. I'm very grateful to God."

The Rogers family, which now numbers thirty-one people, has a long-standing annual family vacation tradition. Orville pays the expenses and, most years, nearly everyone makes it. Last year, it was at a bed & breakfast in Vermont. This year, the family is going on a safari to Kenya and Tanzania. Orville's plan is that all thirty-two of them (there is a baby on the way) will gather for the 2018 USATF Masters Indoor Championships, when he will be one-hundred years old.

There will be a whole new set of records to break in the rarely contested M100 age division. He plans to enter six to seven events in order to set all the records he can. And to have his whole family there cheering for him.

"That's forward thinking," says Orville. "But I like to plan ahead."

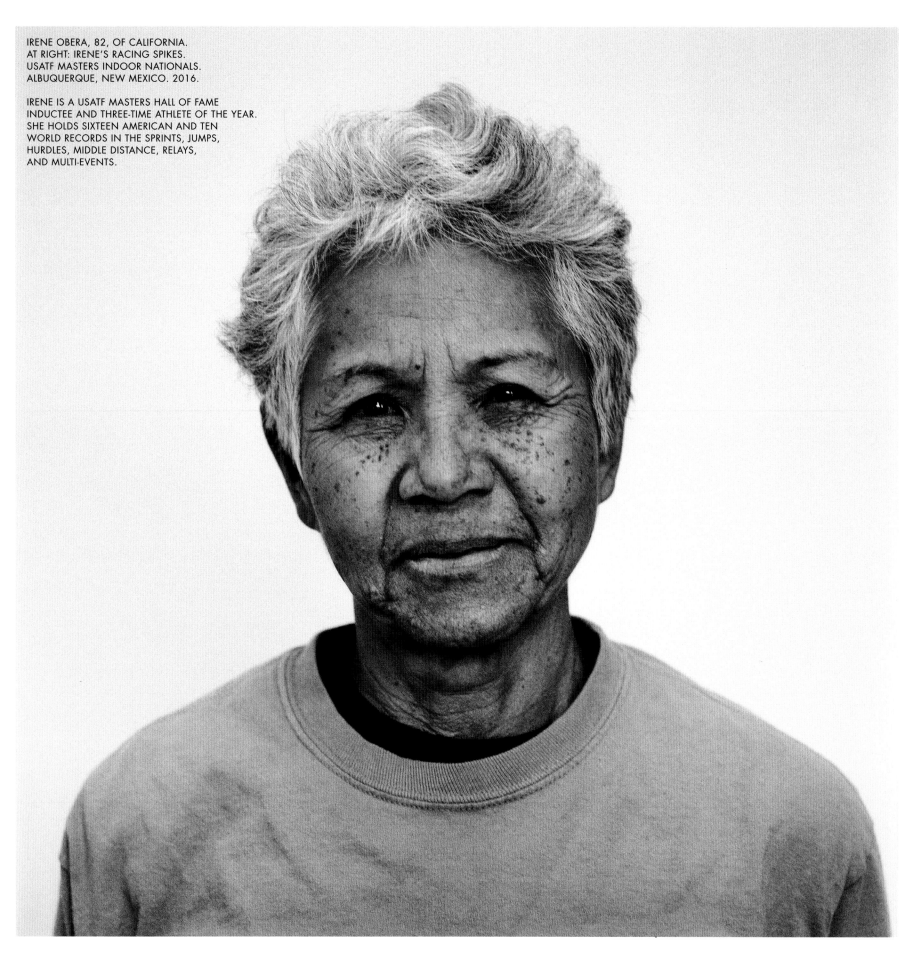

IRENE OBERA, 82, OF CALIFORNIA.
AT RIGHT: IRENE'S RACING SPIKES.
USATF MASTERS INDOOR NATIONALS.
ALBUQUERQUE, NEW MEXICO. 2016.

IRENE IS A USATF MASTERS HALL OF FAME
INDUCTEE AND THREE-TIME ATHLETE OF THE YEAR.
SHE HOLDS SIXTEEN AMERICAN AND TEN
WORLD RECORDS IN THE SPRINTS, JUMPS,
HURDLES, MIDDLE DISTANCE, RELAYS,
AND MULTI-EVENTS.

SUE YEOMANS, 62, GREAT BRITAIN.
POLE VAULT.
WORLD MASTERS.
LYON, FRANCE. 2015.

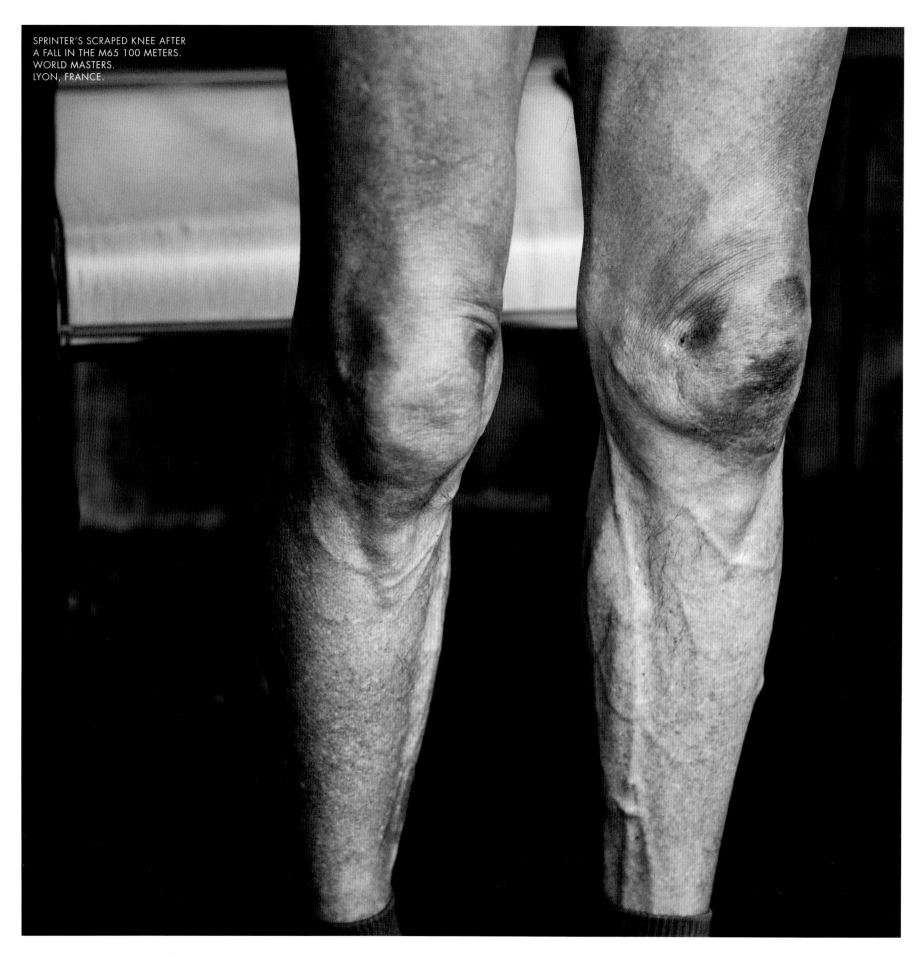

SPRINTER'S SCRAPED KNEE AFTER
A FALL IN THE M65 100 METERS.
WORLD MASTERS.
LYON, FRANCE.

SEYMOUR "SID" DUCKMAN, 88, OF FLORIDA.
HIGH JUMP (.90 METERS/ 2'9½").
AT RIGHT: SUPPORT FROM AN OFFICIAL AND HIS FAMILY
NATIONAL SENIOR GAMES.
LOUISVILLE, KENTUCKY. 2007.

SID, WHO SURVIVED COLON CANCER IN HIS LATE 60S,
PROSTATE CANCER AT 72, AND KIDNEY CANCER AT 80,
HAD JUST UNDERGONE HIS 11TH CHEMOTHERAPY TREATMENT
FOR LUNG CANCER. "I'M A MESS," HE SAID. "BUT I DON'T QUIT."
SID DIED IN 2011.

BARBARA JORDAN, 80, (19.55) BEATS FLO MEILER, 81, (19.56)
BY .01 IN THE W80 100 METERS.
NATIONAL SENIOR GAMES.
ST. PAUL, MINNESOTA. 2015.

Acknowledgements

First and foremost, my deepest gratitude to these masters athletes for sharing your stories for this project. You are champions.

The Racing Age Kickstarter backers made publishing this book possible. A special shout out to my University of Pennsylvania track & field alumni family, whose support accounted for one-third of the funds raised. I appreciate everyone who chipped in at every level; I want to thank all of those who gave at the book level and higher here:

Adria & Brian Sheth, Alanna Sobel, Alex Steffler, Amanda & Robert Chesley, Amanda Heyman, Amy Adams, Andrew Dunlap & Carrie Tatum, April Renae, Ashley Harness, Ashima Jain, Axel Wagner, Betty Costanza, Brett Bonn, Brett Lovins, Brian Peterson, Britt Anderson, Callie Janoff & Randall Stolzfus, Cameron Trimble, Caroline Rebello, Caroline Yang & Leon Wang, Carrie B. Kingsley & Marc Miller, Catherine O'Hern Lyons, Chandra Jessee, Charles Fitt, Chris Jarosch & Brenden Wilde, Chris & Jill Sangster, Christi Strawley, Christina Havenland, Christina Licursi, Christina Schmidlin, Christine Broadhead, Cricket Batz-Shaklee, Dan & Trudy Thompson, Danny & Cassie Tunick, David S. Hosey, Dawn McGee & Marcus Strickland, Delia Vallejo, Denise DeVaan & Elizabeth Bohun, Diana Pizzari, Diane Bassman, Diane Hash, Diane & Scott Peterson, Dionne & Alex Gumbs, Dirk Anschutz, Don & Beverly Isett, Don & Barb Portwood, Doug Murdoch, Douglas Weir, Dr. Denae Wagner & Dr. Kate Hurley, Dravida Consulting, Eleanor Keare, Emily Huber, Erica Sackin, Erik Ling, Eugenia Zukerman, Evan Langenhahn & Kim Ensor, Fernando Pereira Gomes, Flashlight Minneapolis, Gail Danckert, Hans Fex, Herman Milligan & Connie Osterbaan, Ineke Justitz, Jamie DiVenere, Janet Reid, Jenn Lindsay, Jennifer & Dan Butler, Joe Hanlon, John Washburn & Amanda Fox, Jónas Tryggvi Stefánsson, Julie & Dan Morris, Kathleen M. Hayden, Kayla Halleur, Kelley Bussey, Kim & Andrew Purcell, Krista & Andrew Mondschein, Kyle Parker, Landee W. Bryant, Laura Arnold, Leila Navidi, Licia & Tamara Galinsky, Lili Duda, Linda Harness, Linda Stuart, Luana Botelho, Mahala Gaylord, Margaret Keady, Mary & Michael Vanderford, Maureen O'Brien & Sam Nolley, Michael Chico, Michael Rex Schumacher, Michele Markus, Michele Morrissey, Michelle Brady, Michelle & Conner McLaughlin, Mike & Sarah Kinsella, Nadine Goellner & Sarah Foster, Nora & Carlos Tejada, Pattie McCluskey, Polly Jimenez, Preston Merchant, Rebecca Voelkel & Maggie Shannon George, Richard T. Traband, Robert Creighton, Roger Ness, Ron Wainshal, Sara Ator Wilcox, Sarah Charlop-Powers, Sarah Green, Sarah & Fred Kuhnen, Shani Boston, Stella Kramer, Stephen & Alexa Fang, Steve McFarland & Sofie Tholl, Sue & Bruce Bassman, Susan Morison, Suzanne Becker, Ted Swartz, Terri Guinipero, Tessa & Tae Keimes-Kim, Tim Haft, Vanessa Adato & Fernando Maneca, Viragodawg.

Thank you to the fabulous Racing Age creative team who made this book with me:

Ashima Jain, for her elegant design and unrivaled adult trophy collection.

Sarah Foster, for loaning me her Hasselblad for ten years and for bringing her love of running and her beautiful eye to this project.

Ethan Jones of Big Al's, for sticking with this project along its winding path and for producing work of the finest quality at every turn.

David Gardiner Garcia, for handling this challenge with great skill and care.

Becca Tatum for guiding me and not letting me give up.

Winter Miller for the bare-knuckled feedback, surgical triage and heartfelt support.

Robert Frame for the exacting eye.

Thank you to my coaches Betty Costanza, Tony Tenisci, Art Brown and Curtis Tinnin for making me strong.

Thank you for your sponsorship: Mindshift/Think Tank Gear.

A thank you to those who gave me guidance and encouragement in various ways: Andrea Davila, Caroline Yang, Christina Schmidlin, Dewi Lewis, E. Grace Glenny, Heather & Meredith Brislen, Herman Milligan, Houston Fotofest, John Rosengren, Keliy Anderson-Staley, Mani Dravida, Michael Croy, Nadine Goellner, Rixon Reed of Photo Eye, Syd London, Wing Young Huie.

Thank you to the family members, coaches, and friends of the athletes profiled in the book who provided crucial connection, information, and perspective: Bill Rogers, David Gachupin, Jason Patsalis, Mary Harada, Rick Rogers, Stephen Adams, Steven Rogers, Susan Rogers Eveland.

To my fellow photogs who have dedicated themselves to capturing this sport, thanks for what you do: Alex Rotas, David Albo, Eliot Burg, Rob D'Avellar.

A special thank you to Ken Stone for his knowledge and love of the sport and for giving his time, input, and review at various stages of this project.

A special thank you to Kate O'Hern Lyons of the University of Pennsylvania track and field board for her input and support.

Masters track is a labor of love staffed by many people who give their time and expertise with very little compensation to further the mission of the sport. Thanks to Amanda Scotti, Bob Weiner, Sandy Triolo.

Thank you to Laura Roumanos, Sam Barzilay, and Dave Shelley of United Photo Industries for all you do for the world of photography, and for including this work in The Fence exhibit and Brooklyn's Photoville festival. You rock.

Thank you to the writers, editors, curators, gallerists, publications and critics for your interest in, and insight into, this work: Adam Jacques of the *Independent New Review*, Becky Lebowitz Hanger, Jeffrey Furticella, John Leland, and Cornelius Schmid of *The New York Times*, David Rosenberg of *Slate*'s Behold: The Photo Blog, DL Cade of *Petapixel*, Erin Canty of *Upworthy*, Hayley Mac-Millan of *Refinery29*, Jan Nagle and Hannah Frieser of the Center for Photography Woodstock, Jeanette Moses of *American Photo*, Jim Estrin of *The New York Times* LENS Blog, Kaley Sweeney of the *World Photography Organisation Magazine*, Kayla Chobotiuk of *Feature Shoot*, Laurence Cornet of *L'oiel de la Fotografie*, Liam Boylan-Pett of *Runner's World*, Linda Abbit of *Senior Planet*, Marcie Bianco of *Policy Mic*, Margaret Keady of *Newsweek/Daily Beast*, Regina McCombs of *Minnesota Public Radio*, Rick Stet of *HP/De Tijd*, Sarah Foster of Getty Images Creative, Tanya Rynd of Superfine, Thea Traff of *The New Yorker*'s Photo Booth, Yagana Shah of the *Huffington Post*.

Thanks to my lovely neighbor-lords Dan and Trudy Thompson in Minneapolis and to Marya Warshaw and the staff of the Brooklyn Arts Exchange, for the peaceful and creative working and living spaces in which I made this project.

Thanks to the photography organizations that provide me with support and community: ASMP Minneapolis, VisualMN, National Press Photographers Association, W(MN).

To Linda Harness and all the Parkies finding a way to keep moving, we are cheering for you.

Dad, I think you would be really proud of this. Mom, what a brave woman you are. Jess, jumping Jimenezes forever.

Ashley, my love, thank you for being my team, every day.

End Notes

Introduction

1 Arias, Elizabeth. National Vital Statistics Report. Rep. Center for Disease Control, 6 Nov. 2014 and 4 Apr. 2006. Web (accessed 12 Jul. 2016).
2 United Nations, Department of Economic and Social Affairs, Population Division. World Population Prospects: The 2010 Revision, Volume I: Comprehensive Tables. 2011. Web (accessed 1 Mar. 2016).
3 Stone, Ken. "Drug Testing Coming to Regional Meets." MastersTrack.com. 7 Dec. 2015. Web (accessed 12 Jul. 2016).
4 Kremers, Maradit H., et al. Prevalence of Total Hip (THA) and Total Knee (TKA) Arthroplasty in the United States. Proceedings of American Academy of Orthopaedic Surgeons Annual Meeting, New Orleans, Louisiana. 2014.

Johnnye

1 "Tuskegee University — Our History." http://tud1explore. com/2012/10/06/tuskegee-university-our-history/. Tuskegee University, 6 Oct. 2012. Web (accessed 12 Jul. 2016).
2 Chalk, Ocania. *Black College Sport*. New York: Dodd, Mead, 1976. Print.
3 "Nell Jackson." USA Track & Field Masters Hall of Fame Bio. USATF. 1989. Web (accessed 12 Jul. 2016).
4 "Alice Coachman biography." Biography.com. A&E Television Networks. Web (accessed 12 July 2016).

Don

1 Burkett, Brendan, and Gerald A. Carr. *Sport Mechanics for Coaches*. 3rd ed. Champaign, IL: Human Kinetics, 2010. Page 50. Print.

Rita

1 Stone, Ken. "Retired Judge Dick Hanscom Dies at 84." *Times of San Diego*. N.p., 25 Feb. 2016. Web (accessed 12 Jul. 2016).
2 "Men's Pole Vault World Record Progression." Wikipedia, The Free Encyclopedia, 22 Apr. 2016. Web (accessed 1 Jun. 2016).
3 "Women's Pole Vault World Record Progression." Wikipedia, The Free Encyclopedia, 17 May 2016. Web (accessed 1 Jun. 2016).

Nolan

1 Linge, Mary Kay. *Jackie Robinson: A Biography*. Westport, CT: Greenwood Group, 2007. Page 7. Print.
2 "Spinal Stenosis." Ed. David T. Derrer. WebMD Medical Reference, 20 Mar. 2016. Web (accessed 12 Jul. 2016).

Orville

1 "Kenneth H. Cooper, MD, MPH Full Bio." CooperAerobics, n.d. Web (accessed 1 July 2016).

Louise

1 Milberry, Larry, and Hugh A. Halliday. *The Royal Canadian Air Force at War, 1939-1945*. Toronto: Canav, 1990. 149-54. Print.

Tom

1 Patsalis, Jason. "Tom Patsalis highlights." MrTomPatsalis's channel: YouTube. 5 Feb, 2011. Web (accessed 7 July 2016).

David & Tony

1 "19 Pueblos." IndianPueblo.org. Indian Pueblo Cultural Center, n.d. Web (accessed 7 July 2016).
2 "History of the Pueblo of Jemez." JemezPueblo.com. Walatowa Visitor's Center, n.d. Web (accessed 15 June 2016).
3 "New Mexico Boys and Girls State Cross Country Champions." Albuquerque: New Mexico Activities Association, 15 Dec. 2015. PDF.
4 Borzilleri, Meri-Jo. "Almost 40 Years Ago, Steve Gachupin Started an Unmatched Streak of Wins." SkyRunner.com. *Colorado Spring Gazette*, 14 Aug. 2005. Web (accessed 12 July 2016).
5 Jemez Health & Human Services (JHHS)." JemezPueblo. org. Pueblo of Jemez, n.d. Web (accessed 1 June 2016).
6 "Jemez Pueblo: Poverty Status in the Past 12 Months, 2010-2014 American Community Survey 5-Year Estimates." American Fact Finder. United States Census Bureau, 2014. Web (accessed 12 July 2016).
7 Lowe, Sheryl, and Roger Gantz. Overview of the Indian Health Care System. Olympia: Washington State Health Benefit Exchange & Health Care Authority, 1 Apr. 2012. PDF.
8 Gachupin, David. "Jemez Senior Olympians." Pueblo of Jemez, *Walatowa: Red Rocks Reporter*, Oct. 2015. PDF.

Racing Age
Masters track & field athletes redefining the limits of age one jump, throw, and race at a time.

Photography, interviews, and text: Angela Jimenez
Photo editing: Sarah Foster
Scanning and printing: Ethan Jones of Big Al's, Minneapolis
Design: Ashima Jain
Story editor: Winter Miller
Printing: Crystal World Printing Limited, Hong Kong

Angela Jimenez is a visual storyteller based in Minneapolis, Minnesota.
You can find her work at: angelajimenezphotography.com